GREAT DISCOVERIES IN SCIENCE

String Theory

by Meghan Rock

Cavendish
Square
New York

Published in 2017 by Cavendish Square Publishing, LLC
243 5th Avenue, Suite 136, New York, NY 10016

Website: cavendishsq.com

This publication represents the opinions and views of the author based on his or her
personal experience, knowledge, and research. The information in this book serves as a general
guide only. The author and publisher have used their best efforts in preparing this book and
disclaim liability rising directly or indirectly from the use and application of this book.

CPSIA Compliance Information: Batch #CS16CSQ

All websites were available and accurate when this book was sent to press.

Library of Congress Cataloging-in-Publication Data

Names: Rock, Meghan, author.
Title: String theory / Meghan Rock.
Description: New York : Cavendish Square Publishing, [2017] |
Series: Great discoveries in science | Includes bibliographical references and index.
Identifiers: LCCN 2016009002 (print) | LCCN 2016010587 (ebook) |
ISBN 9781502619617 (library bound) | ISBN 150261961X (library bound) |
ISBN 9781502619624 (ebook)
Subjects: LCSH: String models--Juvenile literature.
Classification: LCC QC794.6.S85 R63 2017 (print) |
LCC QC794.6.S85 (ebook) | DDC 539.7/258--dc23
LC record available at http://lccn.loc.gov/2016009002

Editorial Director: David McNamara
Editor: Leah Tallon
Copy Editor: Michele Suchomel-Casey
Art Director: Jeffrey Talbot
Designer: Lindsey Auten
Production Assistant: Karol Szymczuk
Photo Research: J8 Media

The photographs in this book are used by permission and through the courtesy of: Alfred Pasieka/Science Photo Library/Getty
Images, cover, 4; Pasieka/Science Source, 6; iStock, 8; SSPL/Getty Images, 12; iStock, 13; Benjamin D. Esham (bdesham)/File:
Michelson-Morley experiment (en).svg/Wikimedia Commons, 15; Michael Gilbert/Science Source, 22; Science Source, 26;
Encyclopaedia Britannica/UIG via Getty Images, 28; Nina Hernitschek/File: Apfel partikel.jpeg/ Wikimedia Commons, 30; Laguna
Design/Science Source, 33; Encyclopaedia Britannica/UIG via Getty Images, 34; U. S. Library of Congress, 37; MissMJ/Own work
by uploader, PBS NOVA [1], Fermilab, Office of Science, United States Department of Energy, Particle Data Group/File:Standard
Model of Elementary Particles.svg/Wikimedia Commons, 43; iStock, 46; Jakob Emanuel Handmann (1718-1781)/File: Leonhard
Euler 2.jpeg/Wikimedia Commons, 49; CERN Photolab, 51; Acmedogs/File:LeonardSusskindStanfordNov2013.jpeg/Wikimedia
Commons, 53; Bob Paz/Caltech, 56; Ojan/File:Witten at Chalmers.jpeg/Wikimedia Commons, 60; Visuals Unlimited, Inc./Carol
and Mike Wemer/Getty Images, 62; iStock, 69; Laguna Design/Getty Images, 71; Argonne National Laboratory/File: IBM Blue
Gene P supercomputer.jpg/Wikimedia Commons, 74; Lucas Taylor / CERN/http://cdsweb.cern.ch/record/628469/ File:CMS
Higgs-event.jpg /Wikimedia Commons, 76; Agsandrew/Thinkstock, 82; X-Ray: NASA/CXC/J.Hester (ASU); Optical: NASA/
ESA/J.Hester & A.Loll (ASU); Infrared: NASA/JPL-Caltech/R.Gehrz (Univ. Minn.)/ http://www.spitzer.caltech.edu/ images/2857-
sig09-009-NASA-s-Great-Observatories-View-of-the-Crab-Nebula/File:Crab Nebula NGC 1952 (composite from Chandra,
Hubble and Spitzer).jpg /Wikimedia Commons, 84; Steve Jurvetson/ https://www.flickr.com/photos/jurvetson/6971396150/
File:Brian Greene, February 28, 2012.jpg /Wikimedia Commons, 86; Detlev van Ravensswaay/Science Source, 90; Julian
Herzog/ File:CERN LHC Tunnel1.jpg /Wikimedia Commons, 95; Ute Kraus (http://www.uni-hildesheim.de/de/kraus.htm),
Physics education group Kraus, Universität Hildesheim, Space Time Travel (http://www.spacetimetravel.org/), (background
image of the milky way: Axel Mellinger (http://home.arcor.de/axel.mellinger/))/ Gallery of Space Time Travel (http://www.
spacetimetravel.org/galerie/galerie.html)/ File:Black Hole Milkyway.jpg /Wikimedia Commons, 97; stevecoleimages/iStock, 104

Contents

String theorists hypothesize that inside of each of the ball-like particles of the subatomic world is an even smaller strand of vibrating energy. Each strand vibrates in a way that predicts what kind of particle we see it as and, together, the vibrating strings create a kind of symphony.

Introduction

Ever since the ancient Greeks, scientists have wondered what the building block of matter was. If an apple was cut in half, and cut in half again, and cut in half again and again, what would the smallest unit of matter be? So many revelations have been made in the field of physics over the last century. The first was that the atom was the smallest unit of a chemical element, like oxygen. The next was that there were particles within the atom like electrons and protons. The next breakthrough revealed that protons and neutrons were made up of other particles called quarks. Many physicists felt that these were the smallest parts of nature, but string theory takes it all one step further by stating that all these subatomic particles that have been described are actually made of even smaller vibrating strings of energy. This idea is controversial and not supported by all physicists, but it is the very basis of string theory.

One of the greatest controversies of physics today is one that most physicists do not talk about. The Standard Model (the way quantum physicists currently explain the interactions of very small particles) is fatally incompatible with Einstein's theory of general relativity and gravity. The dissonance between these two realms of physics was what Einstein would spend the rest of his life trying to resolve. He searched for what he called the unified theory of everything. Unfortunately for Einstein and modern physics, he was unsuccessful.

String theory is viewed by some of its proponents as the answer to a quest first started by Albert Einstein for a unified theory of everything. It is viewed by its critics as an untestable philosophy and a waste of scientific research money but, in spite of these opposing views, string theory has weathered the advancements in the field for the last forty years.

When physicist Gabriele Veneziano first used Leonhard Euler's beta function to describe the results of particle collisions from accelerators around the world he could never have foreseen where his work would lead. Shortly after Veneziano published his work, other physicists looking at the data realized his equations were describing small strands of energy, or strings. The long road of string theory's development since then has been rocky, at best. For many years the complicated and inconsistent mathematics kept many researchers from dealing with it, but as problems in the equations were resolved, the theory underwent not one but two revelations. String theorists today are hoping for a third that will finally solve the current issues and challenges with string theory.

The fields of quantum physics and cosmology, like the universe itself, are frequently in flux. There are more breakthroughs happening now than ever before thanks to new experimental equipment like special telescopes and larger particle colliders. The push to find a theory of everything that unites Einstein's general relativity and gravity and the world of quantum physics is the driving force behind much of theoretical physics today. While scientists can use one set of equations or the other to describe their subject a majority of the time, there are instances where scientists need both. Black holes and the beginning of the universe require an understanding of quantum physics that integrates gravity to fully explain how they work. String theory currently offers one of the best toolsets to describe these phenomena.

Whether or not string theory will prove correct is a matter of time and more experimentation, but it has a devoted following of scientists willing to put forth this effort. No one can tell what the future will hold for string theory, but its ideas and concepts have already forever changed the field of quantum physics and gravity.

String theory suggests that all particles of matter are stretchy, bouncy, vibrating strings of energy, like subatomic rubber bands.

CHAPTER 1

The Problem of Unifying Physics

Physics, or the study of nature, first got its name in ancient Greece when philosophers began the pattern of observation and hypothesis that scientists still use today. Its definition has been narrowed down since then and is now defined as the study of the universe and how it behaves. Modern physics covers everything from the tiniest parts of matter and how they move to the way universes and galaxies form. But before one can fully understand or even appreciate how profound and strange string theory is, it is important to see what came before it. The evolution of scientific discoveries leading up to string theory has allowed for developments such as Global Positioning System (GPS) and computers, technology that humans have come to use every day.

NEWTON'S LAWS of MOTION

Modern physics began about three hundred years ago with a bright, young student at Cambridge University in England. Isaac Newton contributed to many fields of science and mathematics during his life, such as helping to invent calculus and developing a new type of telescope, but Newton also described the way objects moved. That may not sound like a major accomplishment but Newton's laws of motion form the very basis for modern physics. His works described three laws:

- The law of inertia states that an object at rest will stay at rest unless acted on by another force. It also states that an object in motion will stay in motion unless acted on by another force. Without gravity acting on a ball that one throws, the ball would continue in the direction it was thrown until it ran into something.
- The law of acceleration states that the overall force of an object is equal to the acceleration of the object times its mass. If one threw a Ping-Pong ball and a bowling ball at the same speed, the bowling ball would have more force because it has more mass.
- The law of interactions states that for every action, there is an equal and opposite reaction. If one were to let go of a full balloon, the air rushing out of it would cause the balloon to travel in the opposite direction of the air, with the same amount of force.

These three basic laws are the basis for much of the work that came after Newton, but he didn't stop there. Newton made the connection between an object accelerating here on Earth with the moon's acceleration. With this, Newton became one of the first people to talk about gravity as a universal force. It is the same for us on our planet as it is for planets moving around the sun. Newton concluded that the force that makes an apple from an apple tree accelerate toward the ground is the same force that makes a moon accelerate around a planet. In addition to this, he was able to describe the mathematics precisely. Even with all of the changes modern physics has gone through (like Einstein's theory of gravity), Newton's laws of motion and universal gravitation are still applicable today.

After Newton's work, the world of physics remained quiet for some time. In fact, by the turn of the twentieth century, many scientists felt that the field of physics was completely solved and done, thanks to Newton. It would take many years for people to realize how wrong they were about this. The next spark of scientific revolution took hold with electricity, magnetism, and a man named James Faraday.

ELECTROMAGNETISM and LIGHT

James Faraday did not have any formal schooling, but he was fascinated by all the scientific discoveries he saw happening around him at the turn of the ninetieth century. By apprenticing with scientists working at the time he was able to overcome his lack of schooling, and the training he got was key to his future as a scientist and the discoveries he, himself, would make.

When Faraday started out as a young man, his main interest was in the emerging fields of electricity, or the flow and presence of an electric charge, and magnetism and how the two forces interacted. The flow of electricity is called an electrical current. Magnetism is defined as the ability of an object to repel or attract another object through its electric charge. Though we have these clear definitions of electricity and magnetism now, at the time Faraday studied them, much less was known.

It wasn't until Faraday began experimenting with an iron ring that he really started to advance his understanding of these two forces together. His experiment was simple. He wrapped one wire, connected to a battery, on one side of the ring. On the other side of the ring, he wrapped another wire, connected to a machine that measured electrical current. It may not sound like much, but this experiment would fuel one of his greatest breakthroughs.

Faraday knew that electrical currents measured by other scientists had a magnetic field, the area of how far an object can attract or repel another object through magnetism, around them. He hypothesized that by running an electrical charge through one wire, there would be a measurable current on the other wire. He thought this could happen because of the magnetic field the wires wrapped around the iron ring would create. He wasn't exactly right. A steady current (and steady magnetic field) did not create an electrical charge on the other wire but a change in current—like connecting or disconnecting the battery—created a measurable charge. It came to be called Faraday's law of induction, or the act of one electrical current creating another current through magnetism.

Faraday would continue to experiment using his iron ring and batteries in various ways, but he was hindered. While his experiments were strong, he could not describe the mathematics behind his discoveries. Without these, he had no way to explain how to predict the effects he saw, and other scientists could not test his hypotheses.

Luckily, there was a mathematical prodigy who would come to Faraday's rescue. James Clerk Maxwell was a brilliant

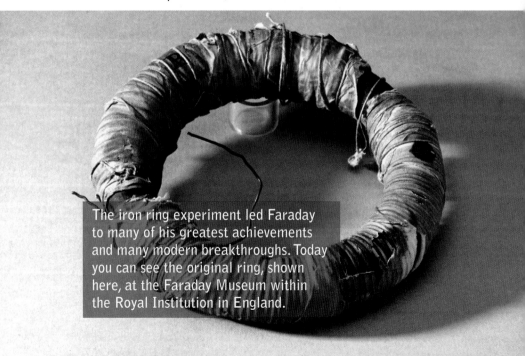

The iron ring experiment led Faraday to many of his greatest achievements and many modern breakthroughs. Today you can see the original ring, shown here, at the Faraday Museum within the Royal Institution in England.

Breakthroughs from the work of Faraday and Maxwell include things like incandescent lighting, electricity in our homes, AM/FM radios, and microwave ovens.

mathematician and, like Faraday, he was fascinated by electricity and magnetism. He was able to write the equations for Faraday's experiments and explain that these two forces were different sides of the same coin.

Maxwell pretty quickly realized something unusual about his equations. What he had dubbed an electromagnetic unit had the speed of 3×10^8 meters per second. Maxwell made the connection between this particular number and the speed of light. He concluded that light could be considered a form of electrical and magnetic waves, but with a shorter wavelength. This meant that light was a form of energy, just like electricity and magnetism. Not only that, it carried a charge, just like the other types of energy they observed. Maxwell's hypothesis that light was a form of electromagnetism was born when his equations predicted what light would do in different situations. With Maxwell's equations and Faraday's experiments to back it up, the electromagnetic theory of light was born, and together they would come to be considered the fathers of modern electromagnetism.

Along with the theory that light was a wave (such as electricity and magnetism) came many questions about how it traveled. Scientists felt that just like water waves needed water to travel through and sound waves needed air, light must need a special medium to transmit these waves. They named this medium luminiferous ether. "Luminiferous" refers to the fact that it relates specifically to light. Even scientists at the time had a hard time explaining ether. As later experiments provided more evidence against it, ether seemed more and more contradictory. Ether was all around us, yet it also had to be massless, invisible, incompressible, and completely uniform. Only light could interact with it. It had to be fluid to fill all of space, yet more rigid than almost any metal so that it could transmit light.

MICHELSON-MORLEY EXPERIMENT

In the summer of 1887 two scientists, Albert A. Michelson and Edward W. Morley, set out to prove the existence of ether. They were trying to determine how Earth moved through this luminiferous ether. Two main hypotheses were being tested. The first was that ether is stationary and Earth partially drags it as Earth moves. The second is that ether is completely dragged along by Earth's movements, which would make the ether appear stationary at Earth's surface.

The setup of the experiment was ingenious. It started by shooting a beam of light. Half of the beam of light was split off by a mirror at a 45° angle. This made half of the beam of light move perpendicular to the rest of it. By splitting a beam of light, Michelson and Morley could measure the speed of light in one direction and a perpendicular direction at the same time. As the light traveled with or against the ether, the speed of light would change.

Not only were their results negative, their experiment was one of the first to disprove the theory of ether. Many scientists

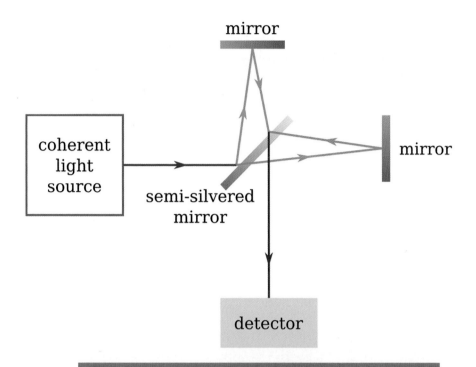

mirror

coherent
light
source

semi-silvered
mirror

mirror

detector

The Michelson-Morley experiment set out to detect the luminiferous ether that was hypothesized to exist. Today it is one of the most famous failed science experiments, and its failure lead Einstein to some of his most important work.

assumed the experiment was flawed or there was something wrong with the equipment that was used but no matter how many times it was repeated or what equipment was used, the results were the same. However, without ether, it was unclear how light traveled through space as a wave, and this is where Einstein would revolutionize physics.

SPECIAL RELATIVITY

Albert Einstein is known worldwide for his genius. In particular, he helped revolutionize the world of physics with several new ideas. Starting in 1905, he would take the world

The Scientific Method

The scientific method is a list of techniques that scientists use to investigate phenomena and acquire new information about the world. In experimental physics, scientists start by making observations about the events they see occurring around them. Then they define a hypothesis about these phenomena. Though scientists can never truly prove a hypothesis, they can reject one. Scientists then performs an experiment to test their hypothesis. If the results do not support the hypothesis, they reject their original hypothesis. More often than not, the results will inspire new observations, and the cycle starts again. As a hypothesis stands the test of all its experiments and cannot be rejected by their results, it is elevated to the status of a theory. A theory is something that has not been disproven by any past experiment and is assumed to be a fundamental way in which the world works.

By contrast, in the field of theoretical physics, scientists use mathematics and models to understand events they observe. In place of a physical experiment in a lab, theoretical physics often use thought experiments to understand things that would be too difficult to test in the laboratory. The theory is evaluated on how well it matches current observations and how well it makes new predictions that can be verified by new observations.

by storm with his novel approaches to the most challenging problems in science at the time. Though James Clerk Maxwell did not realize it at the time, his new electromagnetic theory of light had huge implications. Many physicists realized that the way they understood light did not make sense with these new equations, and they set out to find answers.

According to Newton's laws of motion, people should, in theory, be able to catch up to a beam of light if they were to travel fast enough. Not only could they catch up to light, but its speed should appear different depending on their own motion when they measured it. The Michelson-Morley experiments were a failure in proving the existence of ether. Einstein, however, was the only one to realize they were a success in proving that no matter how you measure light it has the same speed.

Additionally, according to Newton's laws, if you were to run into a beam of light, it would appear faster (your speed plus the speed of light). If you were to run away from a beam of light, it would appear slower (the speed of light minus your speed). Imagine light as an avalanche. If you were to run toward or away from an avalanche, the avalanche would appear faster or slower by your running speed. Yet, in actuality, the speed of light is constant no matter the observer's speed. Einstein set out to explain this conundrum, and in the process he would completely overhaul physics and launch it into the twentieth century.

Albert Einstein was greatly inspired by James Clerk Maxwell's equations. He was also aware of the problems with Maxwell's theory of light and the established Newtonian theory of light. Though he did not know it at the time, many other physicists were struggling with these same problems.

Most other physicists of the time were trying to figure out how the Michelson-Morley experiment was flawed because they felt that ether had to exist. Without ether, how could light travel as a wave as Maxwell predicted and the experiments confirmed? If ether existed it meant the experiment must have been wrong in some way. Einstein's genius came from assuming that if the results were correct, then the idea of ether must be wrong. He suggested that the speed of light was the same no matter how you measured it. This means the speed of light will always be 3 x 10^8 meters/second, no matter your own motion. Therefore, Newton and his ideas must have been wrong. This was and is a revolutionary idea. Imagine that avalanche again. Now imagine no matter how you move away or toward it, its speed remains the same. One of the reasons Einstein's idea was so revolutionary was because of how different it is from our perspective and experience of the physical world. Einstein came to three conclusions. The first is the speed of light is constant, no matter the motion of the observer. Related to this, the second conclusion is the speed of light is the universal maximum speed. Nothing can move faster than the speed of light. The third conclusion he made was that all observations are made relative to the observer's frame of reference and his or her motion. Newton had assumed that it was possible to have an absolute frame of reference in any system, but Einstein realized this was wrong. In order to talk about what you think the movement of another object is, you have to talk about what you believe your own movement to be.

These three different ideas that Einstein had were published in 1905 and came to be called his theory of special relativity. One of the mathematical equations that came out of special relativity is perhaps the most famous science equation, $E=mc^2$. This equation means that energy (E) is equal to mass (m) times the speed of light (c) squared. There is an equivalence between mass and energy. Einstein did not stop at special relativity. His next task was to explain how waves of light can move without ether.

Particle/Wave Duality

Newton first proposed that light was a particle in his work. But in the advent of all of Faraday's work, Maxwell proposed that light was a wave. Neither of these views fully explained all of the experimental results, but each could explain part of those results. Einstein proposed that light, and other electromagnetic waves, had a two-part nature. They could travel as waves, but they could also be particles (like photons and electrons) as well.

Einstein built this proposal on an idea another scientist had in 1900. Max Planck hypothesized that all particles have a specific quantized energy. Einstein theorized that as a wave and a particle light has the same amount (or quanta) of energy. This amount is fixed no matter the form light takes. These two different states behave very differently. For some cases a scientist will have to treat light as a photon in equations. In another circumstance, light would be a wave. He called this combined state of existence the particle/wave duality. A duality refers to the way one event can be viewed in two different ways. Neither state is incorrect as long as both of them are correct. Depending on the circumstance, light can behave as a wave or a particle.

GENERAL RELATIVITY

The papers Einstein published in 1905 made him a household name and cemented his position as one of the greatest minds of the twentieth century. In spite of this, Einstein was troubled. He himself had shown that the speed of light was constant and unsurpassable in the universe. No force should be able to travel faster than this universal speed limit. But gravity appears to act instantaneously across vast distances in space. Einstein could not figure out how this was possible. And he would spend the next ten years of his life working on this problem.

Finally he came to the solution in 1916. He published a paper on what he called the general theory of relativity. He explained that gravity is not a force the way we normally think of it. Gravity is actually a result of an object deforming the fabric of space and time around it. You can actually consider the world around us as having four dimensions: length, width, height, and time. As time can be measured by the length that light takes to travel, you can consider it that fourth dimension but intricately entangled with the three physical dimensions we experience.

Now imagine that space and time form a fabric like you'd find on a trampoline. If something heavy like a bowling ball is placed on the trampoline it would sink down around it. If a golf ball is placed on the same trampoline, it would distort the fabric but only barely. This is why gravity distorts noticeably for big objects like planets and stars, but it distorts less for smaller objects.

This idea of gravity as a distortion of the world around it was a revolutionary concept. Even Newton had not been able to explain how gravity worked, only its equation. With his proposed method for gravity Einstein explained something that not even Newton could.

As revolutionary as Einstein's theory of gravity and general relativity was, it was quickly overshadowed by the developing science of quantum mechanics. Einstein had managed to explain the major force of the universe that we see on the scale of things like planets, stars, and galaxies. But major developments were happening at the same time in the forces seen on the scale of things like atoms and their particle components.

QUANTUM MECHANICS

The same work that inspired Einstein's particle-wave duality allowed the physics of the very small to experience a huge revolution. Max Planck, with his idea of quantized energy, started a new movement in physics that made scientists think about matter on its smallest scale. For thousands of years philosophers hypothesized that all of matter, at its very heart and smallest parts, is made up of individual, indivisible units. But with new tools available scientists could delve more into the tiniest units of matter.

John Dalton, a chemist working at the same time as Faraday, was the first to describe the base unit of an element as an atom. Dalton called it an atom because in Greek atomos means "indivisible." Dalton thought that the atom was the smallest unit of matter in the universe and could not be made smaller. In the 1890s the first subatomic particle, the electron, was found. This meant the atom was not the smallest unit of matter, though it kept its name in spite of this.

The electron was the first subatomic particle described, and the proton and neutron were discovered within the following twenty years. The structure of atoms was determined to be made up of protons, neutrons, and electrons. Protons and electrons both have an electrical charge, but neutrons are electrically neutral. Electrons exist in a mostly empty cloud around the nucleus of the atom. The nucleus is made up of protons and neutrons. From there scientists discovered that protons and neutrons themselves were made of other particles. Today they have described more than a dozen subatomic particles, with many more than that proposed. But neither gravity nor electromagnetism could explain how the nucleus of an atom worked and how protons and neutrons stayed together.

To explain how these subatomic particles were held together to form protons and neutrons, a different kind of force would be needed. Scientists proposed two forces to explain what they observed on the atomic scale. The first is the strong force. This is responsible for holding subatomic particles together to form particles like neutrons and protons. If you are wondering why it is called the strong force, imagine the strength it takes to hold two magnets together with the positive sides facing. Now imagine how hard that is to do times several billion billion billion. This is how strong the strong force is.

The other proposed force related to what scientists witnessed with unstable elements like uranium. They called it the weak force. The weak force is responsible for how the

String theorists believe that quarks and all other elementary particles of matter are made of vibrating strings of energy. The way a string vibrates determines if it will be a quark, or an electron, or even a photon.

FORCE		STRENGTH	RANGE
Strong		1	10^{-15} (diameter of a medium sized nucleus)
Electro-magnetic		$\dfrac{1}{137}$	Infinite
Weak		10^{-6}	10^{-18} (0.1% of the diameter of a proton)
Gravity		6×10^{-39}	Infinite

The four physical forces of our universe are the strong force, the electromagnetic force, the weak force, and gravity. Together these four forces are responsible for the behavior of all matter and energy in the universe.

nucleus decays by emitting different types of subatomic particles. Things like nuclear power and X-rays are related to the weak force.

It wasn't just the forces that were unusual in this newly described world of subatomic particles. The world of the very small is a game of chance. In quantum physics, everything is described as a probability. To describe the location of an electron, physicists give the likelihood of it being in any given area of the atom. This means that on the scale of subatomic particles, the world is chaotic and driven by probability.

At our scale, physicists riding in a car can say exactly how fast the car is going and what their location is. However, to describe the state of a subatomic particle like its speed or location you have to fire another particle at it. By firing this second particle, you change the first particle's state. So at any given time you can only describe approximate location and speed. The more accurately you can describe one, the less accurately you can describe the other. This became known as Heisenberg's uncertainty principle, after Werner Heisenberg, the man who described it.

Together the strong and weak forces and things like the uncertainty principle came to explain much of what was observed in this new world of quantum physics. On the scale of the very small, physicists were able to describe many of the strange experimental results with great accuracy. But the trouble came when gravity was included in their equations.

The HOLES in OUR KNOWLEDGE

Einstein quickly realized that gravity could not be incorporated with the equations of the strong and weak forces. He would spend the last thirty years of his life tirelessly searching for a unified theory of everything, or theory of the four forces of nature. Unfortunately, not even Einstein's genius could solve the problem. The hole in our knowledge that string theory seeks to resolve is how the four forces work all together.

In modern physics we have two sets of physical laws. Quantum mechanics and general relativity predict and explain the things we observe with great accuracy within their own scales. Electromagnetism and the weak and strong forces all work together seamlessly on the scale of atoms and subatomic particles. Gravity and general relativity are astoundingly precise when it comes to explaining how extremely massive things, like planets and stars, act in the universe.

But if you try and combine the equations of general relativity and quantum physics you get nonsense answers. Imagine inputting 2 + 2 into your calculator and getting the answer "a fish riding a bicycle with a mustache." So even today there is no unified set of equations that explains the universe as a whole. This is where the current theories fall short. They fail to address this because gravity is very difficult to explain on the small scale, and the way particles interact is unimportant on the scale of humans and planets.

For most of the things physicists study it is only necessary to use the equations for subatomic particles or the equations for gravity. Very rarely do you have something small or fast enough and also massive enough to need both sets of equations. But when physicists want to understand an event like the start of the universe as we know it, or how a black hole works, they need both sets of equations.

The fatal inconsistencies of gravity and quantum mechanics leave physicists in a tough spot. Starting with Faraday and Maxwell unifying electricity and magnetism, the world of physics has been a waltz that continues to split and come back together. Einstein and general relativity and Planck and quantum mechanics have danced around each other for the last century. The next great challenge in physics will be unifying these two fields. The insights that come out of this unification may lead to things that seem to come straight off the pages of a science fiction novel.

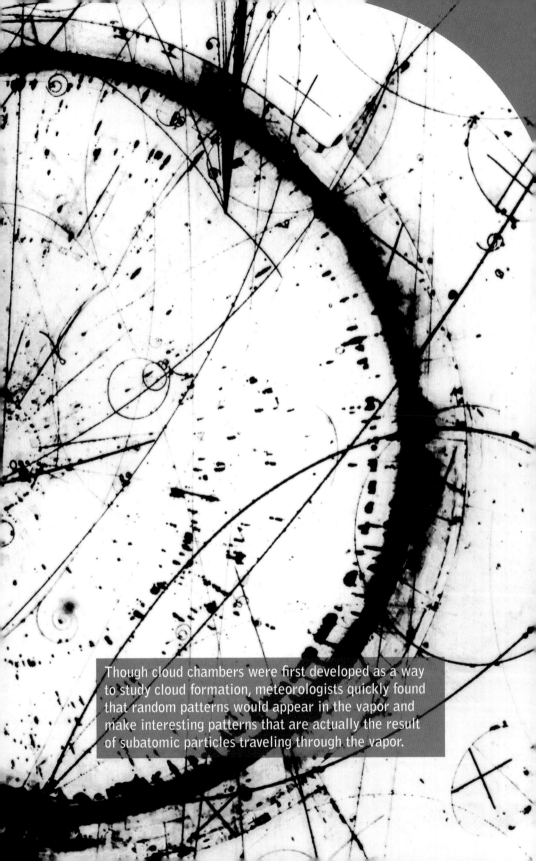

Though cloud chambers were first developed as a way to study cloud formation, meteorologists quickly found that random patterns would appear in the vapor and make interesting patterns that are actually the result of subatomic particles traveling through the vapor.

CHAPTER 2

The Science Behind String Theory

There are a few building blocks of physics that one needs to grasp before learning about string theory. The building blocks necessary to understand string theory are atomic structure, the types of subatomic particles currently described, and the four fundamental forces of physics. The current model to explain three of these fundamental forces is the Standard Model, but it does not include gravity. The theory of general relativity and the Standard Model are incompatible, and string theory hopes to bridge the gap between them.

The STRUCTURE of ATOMS

To understand much of what the four forces do, one needs to understand the structure of atoms. The current understanding of the atom's structure all began when electrons were first discovered in the 1890s using a cathode ray. A cathode ray is a glass tube where almost all the gases have been removed. This means the inside of a cathode ray is a vacuum, like space. On each end of the cathode tube is a metal plate. One plate is positive and one plate is negative. If you connect a charge to each of the plates, the charge will flow through the tube. By applying

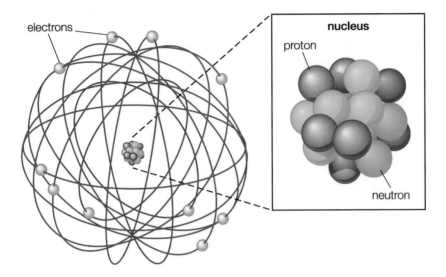

electrons

nucleus

proton

neutron

Scientists figured out through experimental results that very small, negatively charged particles orbited around a nucleus made of positively and neutrally charged particles. The electrons and protons, together, are responsible for the electrical charge of an atom. The protons and neutrons are primarily responsible for the mass of an atom.

a magnetic field to the tube, scientists were able to show that the beam was attracted to the positive, meaning it was negative. You could even use a magnet to deflect the beam of energy flowing through a cathode tube. So even though there was nothing inside the tube to transmit the electricity, it managed to move. Scientists realized there was a negatively charged electric particle much smaller than an atom that was responsible for transmitting electric energy. They called it an electron.

It has taken many years to figure out the structure of an atom, but scientists have discovered there are three components. On the outside there are very small negatively charged particles called electrons (discovered first in the cathode ray experiments). Further experimentation showed that at the center of the atom is a nucleus. The nucleus of an atom is made up of protons and neutrons. Protons have a positive charge but 1,836 times the mass of an electron. The neutrons in the nucleus of the atom are electrically neutral and slightly larger than the protons. Together, the protons and neutrons are responsible for almost all the mass of an atom. For every proton in the nucleus there is a corresponding electron in orbit around the nucleus. So in its natural state as a whole an atom should be electrically neutral.

The number of protons in the nucleus of the atom is what makes the atom a particular element on the periodic table. An element is a substance that cannot be broken down into simpler substances by chemical means. For instance, water can be broken down into hydrogen and oxygen atoms. But oxygen cannot be broken down into any simpler compounds by chemical means. Therefore, oxygen is an element, water is not. Neutrons do not define a particular element like protons, but there is often an average number of neutrons that occur in the nucleus of each element.

Fundamentally, electrons repel other electrons and are attracted to protons. Neutrons are neutral and have no attraction or repulsion to either protons or electrons. The attraction between protons and electrons is stronger the closer the electrons are to the nucleus. The larger an element is, the more electrons it has (there is one electron for every proton in the nucleus). As an element has more electrons, they get farther from the nucleus in the electron cloud around it. The looseness that these outer electrons experience, or how likely it is that they could leave the atom, is what makes electromagnetism possible.

SUBATOMIC PARTICLES

Subatomic particles were rapidly discovered over the last century. Once Einstein and Planck postulated the existence of the quantized photon, new particles were quickly hypothesized.

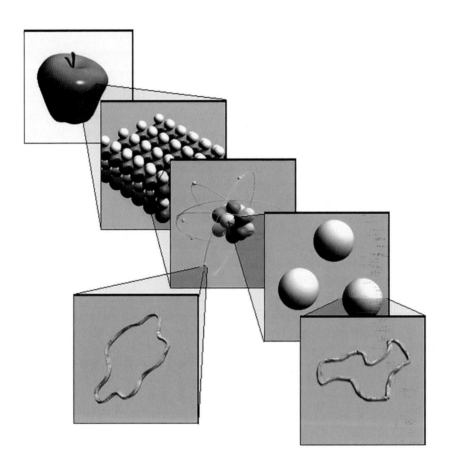

Scientists know the skin of an apple to be made of an assemblage of atoms in the form of molecules. Found within the atom are electrons, protons, and neutrons. Recent experiments with particle colliders have shown that some of these subatomic particles can be broken down even further into quarks.

Scientists sometimes jokingly refer to the wide array of subatomic particles as the subatomic zoo because there are so many.

Particles have several characteristics, depending on the type of particle . These characteristics include spin, electric charge, potential mass, and color charge. The color charge in quantum physics is not color like one sees in a rainbow, but color as a way of categorizing a new property of particle interactions. Spin refers to the angular momentum of a particular particle. Just like the planet spins, the particles and subatomic particles we will talk about also spin, but in a different way. On the quantum scale, it can sometimes take two rotations to come back to where you started originally. Particles either spin in whole numbers (0, 1, or 2) or they spin with 1/2 integer spin.

The first way to break it down is into the two major classes of particles: fermions and bosons. Fermions are particles of matter and make up the world around us. Bosons, or gauge bosons, are the carriers of force for the four fundamental forces of the universe. Together both types of particles are responsible for everything in the universe and the way all matter reacts.

Fermions

The defining characteristic of fermions is they all have 1/2 integer spin. Beyond that, they all have mass (making them the building blocks of matter). They are capable of having positive or negative electric charge, but there are several fermions with no charge. There are three types of fermions: quarks, leptons, and hadrons. Only quarks are capable of having color charge because quarks are the only fermion that interacts using the strong force (covered later in this chapter). All fermions, except for neutrinos, also have an antiparticle, which is a particle with all the same spin but opposite electrical and color charges. Antiparticles annihilate when they meet their particle twin and create bursts of energy, destroying both the particle and antiparticle.

There are six different varieties of quarks, called flavors. They include up, down, bottom, top, strange, and charm. Because they join together using the strong force to form composite particles, they also have fractional charge (-1/3 or +2/3). We do not see their fractional charges because when they are a part of a hadron they have a whole integer charge like +1 or 0. Quarks are never observed outside of their composite particles.

The leptons also have six flavors. The electron, muon, and tau particles are all leptons. For each of these there is also a corresponding neutrino: the electron neutrino, the muon neutrino, and the tau neutrino. The muon and tau particles are quite large compared to the electron, but the neutrinos are all much smaller than their sister particle. Leptons do not interact through the strong force so they have no color charge.

Hadrons are the final group of fermions. These are composite particles made up of quarks or particles and their antiparticles. Composite particles made up of quarks, called baryons, include the neutron and proton we see in the nucleus of the atom. Mesons are shorter lived because they contain a quark and its antiquark. They quickly break down and release leptons in the process. Many particle accelerators, like the Large Hadron Collider, focus on using hadrons to explain subatomic particle interactions.

Bosons

Bosons are responsible for carrying the four fundamental forces of the universe. They are defined by having whole integer spin. Depending on the particle, they can have mass or be massless. The only electrically charged bosons are the W+ and W- bosons responsible for the weak force. A theory

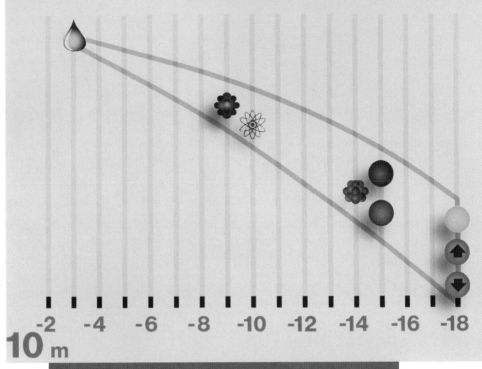

-2 -4 -6 -8 -10 -12 -14 -16 -18
$10^{}$ m

A water droplet is 1,000,000,000,000,000, or a quadrillion, times larger than the quarks that make up the protons that make up the atoms that make up the water molecules inside of it.

that uses bosons to explain force interactions is called a gauge theory. Gluons are the only bosons with color charge as this is a property of only particles that interact through the strong force. For all bosons except the W bosons, they are their own antiparticle. This has been proven in particle collider experiments. When a photon interacts directly with another photon, they annihilate each other. For the W- boson, the antiparticle is the W+ boson and vice versa.

There are six types of bosons that have been confirmed to exist so far. Photons are the gauge boson of the electromagnetic force. They are massless and electrically neutral. They were also the first boson to be hypothesized. The W+, W-, and Z gauge bosons are all responsible for the weak force. These bosons have more than eighty-three times the mass of the proton

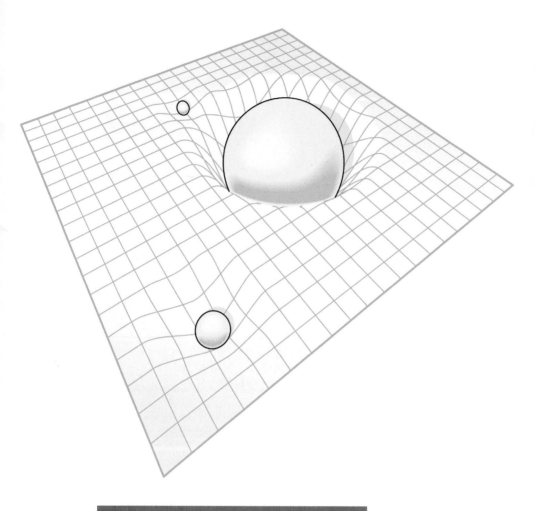

The easiest way to imagine Einstein's theory of gravity involves a stretchy two-dimensional plane, like the top of a trampoline. On top of this stretchy plane are different-sized spheres. Here, the largest and most massive sphere distorts the surface the most. The two smaller spheres distort the surface as well, but not as much because they are less massive.

or neutron in the nucleus. Gluons are a massless particle responsible for the strong force. They are the only boson with color charge. The final boson that has been discovered is the Higgs boson. It is not responsible for a fundamental force like the bosons already described but is the force carrier for mass. Other particles, like quarks and leptons, have mass because of interactions with Higgs bosons. They are the most massive of all the bosons. They are also the only bosons with 0-spin.

The final boson that is proposed and has yet to be discovered is the graviton. This does not worry scientists very much because it took almost sixty years for the Higgs boson to finally be confirmed by experiments. Because of the graviton's properties it will be even harder to find and detect. The graviton is responsible for the fundamental force of gravity. Richard Feynman, a famous theoretical physicist, is the scientist who theorized that if it does exist, it would be a massless particle with 2-spin.

The FOUR FORCES

There are four fundamental forces of the universe that scientists have found. They are sometimes called the fundamental interactions because they relate to how matter interacts with other matter. The first is probably the one most people are familiar with: gravity. Going up in strength is the weak nuclear force. The weak nuclear force is responsible for things like radioactive decay. The second strongest interaction is the electromagnetic force, though it is billions of times stronger than gravity. This is the force responsible for making electric lights, computers, and anything that needs electricity to run. The strongest force only happens on the scale of subatomic particles: the strong force. All together these four forces explain the way all of the matter in the universe interacts.

We can also think about these fundamental interactions in terms of "fields" or limited areas of space where that force is

Albert Einstein

Albert Einstein's first major papers were published in 1905. He was a relatively unknown scientist at this point, but he would not be for long. Working from a Swiss patent office, he revolutionized physics. His is considered some of the most important work that has been done in the field of physics in the last two hundred years. Einstein's theory of the particle/wave duality and his theories of relativity rocked the scientific community. In his first four papers he was able to explain things that had stumped most of his fellow scientists.

He would pave the way for scientists studying everything from subatomic particles to black holes and the beginning of the universe. Unfortunately he found the jittery, chaotic nature of subatomic particles in the quantum world to be unpleasant and deeply unsettling. He spent most of the later part of his life searching for a way to unite all four forces of physics into a single theory. In spite of his brilliance and dedication, Einstein was not able to see this goal accomplished in his lifetime. Today modern physicists have carried on with Einstein's work, and string theory may be the best choice for a unified field theory.

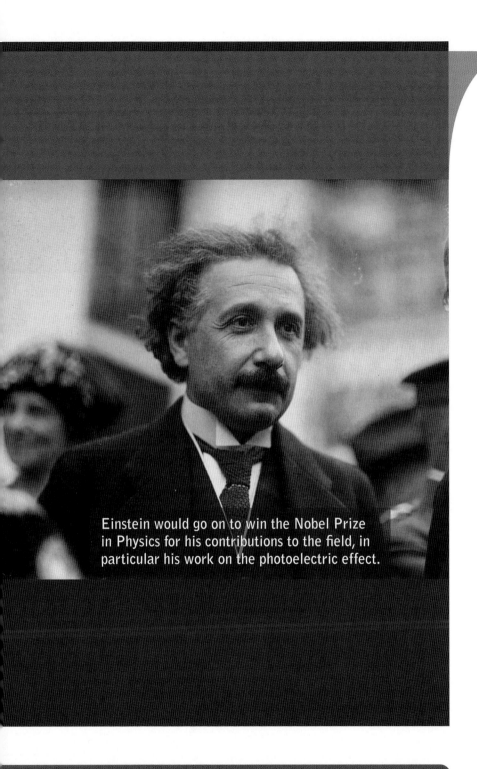

Einstein would go on to win the Nobel Prize in Physics for his contributions to the field, in particular his work on the photoelectric effect.

active. Gravity has the largest field of effect. The nuclear forces, the weak and strong forces, are only really active on the scale of atoms and subatomic particles.

The Gravitational Force

Though it is hard to imagine to those that experience it daily, gravity is the weakest of the forces. If the strength of gravity is one, the strong force by comparison would be a one followed by thirty-nine zeroes. It makes sense because if gravity were stronger than the other forces, a person would be pulled through the floor of his or her house, through the surface of the planet, and down to its very core! Thanks to the strength of the electromagnetic force and the nuclear forces, a person is able to stand on the floor because the atoms of his or her shoes repel the atoms of the floor.

Newton first talked about gravity when he was making his laws of motion (see chapter 1). He defined gravity as the force attracting two objects toward each other. The strength of the attraction increases when the mass of either object increases. The strength of the attraction decreases with greater distance between the objects. Though Newton was able to describe the equation for gravity, he could not explain why it worked.

Einstein explained gravity first by combining the four dimensions of space and time (one of time, three of space). The combined dimensions, called space-time, could be thought of like a piece of fabric covering the universe. The fabric of space-time is like the fabric of a trampoline. When something very massive like a star or planet is on the fabric of space-time, the fabric distorts around the object. A smaller object, like a human, would only barely distort the surface.

Imagine a person in a rocket ship here on Earth. Thanks to Earth's gravity, the person feels pulled toward the floor of the rocket ship. Imagine that same person traveling in the rocket ship deep in outer space, without any source of gravity around. If the rocket ship is accelerating, the person would feel pulled toward the floor of the ship, the same way he or she felt under the influence of Earth's gravity. This is how Einstein likened gravity to acceleration. Einstein and Newton both understood that gravity was about acceleration, but by using space-time Einstein could explain why it worked. The gravitational force, according to Einstein, is really an object accelerating toward the dip in the fabric of space-time left by another object.

In this way, all four dimensions are distorted by large objects, including time. Everything is affected by the dips and valleys of space-time's fabric, including light, even though it has no mass. The first confirmation of space-time and Einstein's new idea of gravity was during a solar eclipse in 1919. Scientists knew what stars should be hidden directly behind the sun at this point in the year. If Einstein's space-time and gravity were correct, light from those stars behind the sun would be visible as it moved around the distortion of space-time the sun made. And light from those hidden stars was visible at the edges of the eclipse! The light coming from these stars was bent by the sun's gravity. Or, more accurately, according to Einstein, the sun's distortion of space-time. On top of that, the light was bent by exactly the amount Einstein predicted.

The hypothetical subatomic particle that would carry the force of gravity is called a graviton. Though it has been predicted by physicists, no experiment has yet been able to prove its existence. If it did exist, it would be a gauge boson like the other force-carrying particles. While scientists have not observed it, mathematical equations by Feynman show it would be a massless particle with spin-2. This will be important in chapter 3 when string theory becomes a theory of gravity.

The Electromagnetic Force

Electromagnetism is the next force that was described in the world of physics. Electromagnetism is the range of physical effects involving electrically charged particles in motion or at rest. It is a complicated force to explain because one characteristic (electrical charge) is responsible for so much of the world around us, not just electricity and magnetism. At its heart, electromagnetism relates to the way an atom is structured and the "charge" the different parts of the atom have. Electrons and protons and their opposing charges are the driving force behind electromagnetism.

At first, electricity and magnetism were considered to be two separate forces. However, thanks to the work of James Faraday and the equations of James Clerk Maxwell, scientists realized that they were related forces. Electromagnetism is a fundamental force of interaction that happens between particles with electrical charge.

Today we know that both electricity and magnetism work because of structures within the atom. Currently we define electricity as the flow and presence of electric charge. Atoms can hold a negative or positive electric charge depending on the number of electrons versus the number of protons in the atom. Atoms can also pass along charge to each other and allow for the flow of this charge by passing along electrons. There are two types of electricity: static electricity and electrical current. Static electricity is what makes a balloon you've rubbed on your head stick to a wall.

The electricity of electrical current is caused by the flow of electrons from one atom to the next. This flow of electrons occurs better in larger atoms with many electrons. In larger atoms, the outer electrons are further away from the nucleus and have more freedom. Electricity starts by running charge through a positive plate. Electrons are attracted to this positive charge, and then one side of an atom has a slightly more positive charge and attracts the electrons of other atoms near it. Electrons of the nearby atoms move toward the more positive area. This creates a new positive spot on the atom the electrons just moved away from. All these atoms aligning in a chain reaction create both electrical current and a magnetic field around the wire. The aligning of the atoms is called polarization. Polarization is also required to create a magnet. When the atoms are polarized like this, the flow of electrons happens very easily from one atom to the next. The greater the flow of electrons, the greater the electric energy is. Electrical energy can flow through anything that can carry electrical charge. Whole atoms, like electrically charged ions (how our nervous system works), or individual electrons will all carry electrical energy.

Electromagnetism does not just allow our computers to be powered. It is how our nervous system works, and it is responsible for all of chemistry. This bioelectricity allows information to be carried along our nervous system so we can think and so we can move our bodies. The chemical bonds of molecules form through attractions between different atoms' protons and electrons.

Photons are called the force carrier particles of electromagnetism because they only interact with charged particles, not with themselves. They exert electromagnetic forces on electrically and magnetically charged particles. Thanks to the work of Faraday and Maxwell, scientists now know that photons themselves are a form of electromagnetic waves.

The Weak Force

While the other forces are about how things come together in their interactions, the weak force is more about how things come apart. The weak force is responsible for things like nuclear decay.

There are three particles that carry the force for the weak interaction: the W^+, W^-, and Z bosons. The W^+ and W^- bosons are responsible for nuclear decay. By expelling a W^- boson, a neutron can turn into a proton. This reaction also results in the release of energy (and an electron neutrino) that we see as nuclear radiation. By creating protons from neutrons, new elements are created. The weak force is also the primary way in which neutrinos interact with other matter. Since neutrinos have no electric charge and are not responsive to the strong force, the only way they can interact is through gravity and the weak force. The Z boson is how most of these neutrino interactions occur.

The W and Z bosons are also extremely massive. The W bosons are eighty-three times the size of the proton, and the Z boson is ninety-three times the size of the proton. This makes them HUGE in comparison to almost all other subatomic particles. To put it in perspective, if a neutron were about the size of a pug, the W bosons would be about the size of a water buffalo. The weak force is limited by the massive size of its particles. Its strength shrinks to almost zero beyond the radius of a single proton. You might wonder how it is possible for the neutron to spit out a particle that is eighty-three times heavier than the neutron itself. This is because (thanks to Einstein's work) we know that mass and energy are equivalent through the equation $E=mc^2$. The particle that is spat out is made purely of the converted energy from the neutron itself—the W boson was never actually in the neutron in a physical mass form, only in the form of energy. Because the amount of energy is so large, the W boson released can be extremely massive.

The weak force is primarily responsible for nuclear fusion, our ability to use techniques like radiocarbon dating, and neutrino interactions. The only force weaker than it is gravity. The weak force is the force that keeps stars burning and causes radioactive decay.

The Strong Force

The appropriately named strong force is the strongest of all four forces. It is responsible for holding quarks together to form hadrons like protons and neutrons. The residual strength of

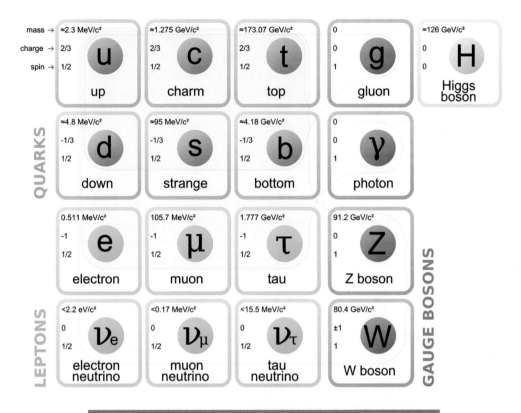

mass →	≈2.3 MeV/c²	≈1.275 GeV/c²	≈173.07 GeV/c²	0	≈126 GeV/c²
charge →	2/3	2/3	2/3	0	0
spin →	1/2	1/2	1/2	1	0
	u	c	t	g	H
	up	charm	top	gluon	Higgs boson

QUARKS

	≈4.8 MeV/c²	≈95 MeV/c²	≈4.18 GeV/c²	0	
	-1/3	-1/3	-1/3	0	
	1/2	1/2	1/2	1	
	d	s	b	γ	
	down	strange	bottom	photon	

	0.511 MeV/c²	105.7 MeV/c²	1.777 GeV/c²	91.2 GeV/c²	
	-1	-1	-1	0	
	1/2	1/2	1/2	1	
	e	μ	τ	Z	
	electron	muon	tau	Z boson	

LEPTONS

	<2.2 eV/c²	<0.17 MeV/c²	<15.5 MeV/c²	80.4 GeV/c²	
	0	0	0	±1	
	1/2	1/2	1/2	1	
	ν_e	ν_μ	ν_τ	W	
	electron neutrino	muon neutrino	tau neutrino	W boson	

GAUGE BOSONS

The different subatomic particles are broken down here into three main groups: quarks, leptons, and gauge bosons. The bosons all have whole integer spin, and the quarks and leptons all have half integer spin.

this force is also responsible for keeping neutrons and protons together in the nucleus. If you remember from before, a bunch of positively charged particles really should repel each other rather than forming into a tightly bound nucleus of an atom. The strong force has a charge, but rather than an electrical charge, we call it a color charge. It is important to remember that the strong force's color charge is not really like the color we see due to light waves. Color charge is more a way of explaining the three different charged states quarks and gluons can have and the various mixes the particles can make. The three basic color charges are red, green, and blue. The charges can mix together readily as quarks form new hadrons and interact with gluons and each other. Quarks are the only fermions that have color charge and the only particles that respond directly to the strong force. The particle of force that carries the strong force is the gluon. It is named that because it is the glue that holds quarks together. It can also interact with itself to form a proposed particle called a "glueball" where no quarks are present, but it has not been detected experimentally yet.

The strong force is the reason we have matter. Without gluons holding together quarks we would have no protons or neutrons. Without the residue of gluons holding together protons and neutrons we would have no nuclei in the heart of our atoms. The strong interaction is the most essential force for the existence of matter as we know it because it holds together atoms.

The STANDARD MODEL

The current way of explaining the way the forces all work together is the Standard Model. The physicists responsible for discovering it went on to win the Nobel Prize in Physics in 1979. In fact, much of the chapter's explanation of subatomic particles relies on hypotheses made by the Standard Model that were confirmed by experimental results.

The only problem is this model is incapable of allowing for quantum gravity. To date, no one has been able to make the equations of the Standard Model work if there is any kind of gravity included. This is fairly troublesome for physicists because if a theory were correct you should be able to include gravity without it breaking down. Unfortunately, Einstein's general relativity and the Standard Model are fatally incompatible.

The search for a unified theory that includes quantum gravity (gravity on the scale of other atoms) is the holy grail of physics quests. While it isn't needed for many equations, scientists need gravity and quantum physics to understand things that are both very tiny and very massive, like black holes and the big bang.

String theorists hope that string theory will be a unified theory of everything, uniting all four physical forces. There are signs that it may indeed be a good candidate for the theory of everything but many physicists still have doubts about this.

The outside of the aboveground main building at the Large Hadron Collider. This building is the headquarters for the European Organization for Nuclear Research, or CERN. It is currently the most powerful and largest particle collider in the world.

CHAPTER 3

The Major Players in String Theory

O ne of the most exciting things about string theory is that it's a group effort. Lots of mathematicians and scientists around the world have made profound contributions. String theory is so compelling that its development is the story of more than any one person, group, or even university. Thousands of people worked tirelessly to bring string theory to where it is today. We can narrow down pivotal people in string theory by looking at the different revolutions of string theory. At the center of each breakthrough is a great mind in physics. Many of the people in this chapter would go on to win Nobel Prizes for their contributions to the field of physics. In addition to the researchers in the field, we also have to acknowledge several important figures for public education on string theory.

PRE-STRING THEORY

Euler's Beta Functions

The first person we can talk about being important to string theory lived more than two hundred years ago, believe it or not. Leonhard Euler (1707–1783) was born in Switzerland and was originally planning to be a clergyman like his father. However, early in his studies his tutors realized he had a brilliant mind, and they encouraged him to pursue a career in academics. Euler went to college at the age of thirteen. By the age of sixteen he had his master's degree and was being personally tutored by another one of history's greatest mathematicians, Johann Bernoulli.

Euler wrote all his life, and today we have more than thirty thousand pages of his work and notes. He is known for proposing many different forms of mathematical notation, like $f(x)$ for functions in algebra and using π to denote pi. With all this writing he created a set of equations, called Euler beta functions, that are mostly used for pure mathematics. These equations would go unstudied for many years, but without Euler's work string theory would likely not exist today. His beta functions were known by many, but it would take a new mind to see their potential.

Twentieth-Century Physics

The work of various physicists at the start of the twentieth century would cause a revolution in the field of physics. From understanding how gravity worked by warping the space-time around it to understanding the parts of an atom, physicists were learning all about the worlds of the very small and very large. With the advent of the nuclear bomb and splitting the atom, scientists began to focus on quantum physics, the study of very small particles making up the atom. Deep within all the matter around us is a hidden world, and scientists were determined to find out more.

By the mid-twentieth century scientists were using particle accelerators to smash different atoms into each other to see what happened. When you smash particles into each other at such high speeds, there is a spray of particles released. Sometimes physicists compare this to taking a hammer to something as hard as you can to see what it's made of by

This 1756 oil painting of Leonhard Euler was created by Jakob Emanual Handmann when Euler was forty-nine. At this point in his life he had written two of his most important works (on mathematical functions and differential calculus) and was renowned for his mathematical mind and prowess.

looking at all the pieces that are left over afterward. Because they make up only a part of the atom scientists called the leftover shards of atoms subatomic particles.

The results of the particle accelerator experiments created many new ideas about how our universe worked on the scale of the very tiny and what was happening deep inside the atom. The main effort of physicists at this time was aimed at explaining how these subatomic particles scattered after the collisions in the particle accelerators.

Veneziano Dual Resonance Model

There is a long gap between Euler and the next important figure of string theory. This is where we find a young Italian scientist, Gabriele Veneziano (1942–), working at CERN, the newly formed particle accelerator lab in Europe. It was an exciting time to be working there. Many of his colleagues were working on the results of the new particle accelerator experiments. They all were trying to explain the way particles in the nucleus interacted with each other. This is when Veneziano realized that Euler's equations could explain the experimental results.

Veneziano found that Euler's equations came surprisingly close to explaining how strongly interacting particles, like those in a particle accelerator, behave. In addition, the mathematics were simple and beautiful. In physics, often the elegant mathematical equations that explain reality well end up being correct. Veneziano called it the dual resonance model, and it made history. After he published his work there was an explosion of people looking at Euler and the dual resonance model to explain how particles interacted. Without Veneziano making the connection between his work at CERN and the mathematics of Leonhard Euler there would be no string theory to talk about today.

Unfortunately, the dual resonance model was close but not perfect. The problem was no parts of the equation could be

Gabriele Veneziano was responsible for leading the way to string theory. His work connecting Euler's beta functions with the modern experimental results of particle colliders laid the groundwork for string theorists to come.

changed. In physics you should be able to change one or two parts of an equation slightly. The results of your changes will create a different result, but the equation itself should still be valid.

When physicists tried to tinker with Veneziano's model to add in new values and make the results more accurate, the equations collapsed. Veneziano built a house of cards with Euler's math. No one could change or add new cards without causing the whole structure to collapse. It was suggested by some that there were no changes you could make to the equation without a complete break down of the mathematics. This meant nothing could be done to make the Veneziano model more closely resemble the experimental results.

BOSONIC STRING THEORY

Three physicists came up with the idea that founded string theory. They were all young professors and very enthralled with the dual resonance theory. Yoichiro Nambu (1921–2015) was a Japanese physicist working at the University of Chicago. Meanwhile in Denmark at the Niels Bohr Institute, Holger Nielsen (1941–) was working with the Veneziano model as well. In America, Leonard Susskind (1940–) of Stanford University had a similar idea to his colleagues Nambu and Nielsen. All three of these men published the idea, starting in 1970 with Nambu, that Veneziano's model was actually describing small, vibrating strings of energy. If the strings were very, very small then they would seem like points of matter as the experiments seemed to show. There was a brief bit of excitement in the physics world about this new bosonic string theory but it would die off quickly.

There were several problems that seemed insurmountable for bosonic string theory. The first was that it didn't allow for particles like electrons to exist. The second was that the math required the existence of twenty-six dimensions. To put this in perspective, humans experience three dimensions of space (length, width, and depth) and one of time. Twenty-six dimensions was beyond most people's comprehension. The final problem of bosonic string theory was the particle it predicted that could move faster than light. With all these challenges facing it, it is a wonder that any form of string theory survived at all.

Meanwhile, other physicists came up with the theory of quantum chromodynamics. This better explained the results from the particle accelerator experiments than bosonic string theory. The problem that Veneziano originally set out to solve, how particles interacted, appeared to be solved by this new model. With the development of quantum chromodynamics and an explanation of particle interactions, many people stopped working on Veneziano's model and string theory altogether.

One major problem with the dual resonance model and bosonic string theory is they only allowed for bosons. Bosons are particles that are usually responsible for carrying forces in the quantum world. Forces are things like the electromagnetic force and the weak and strong nuclear forces. For instance, the photon is the electromagnetic force's boson. But there is more to quantum physics than just forces. There has to be something for forces to act upon: particles of matter. Fermions are these particles of matter. Without fermions like electrons and protons, we would have no physical world. So the fact that bosonic string theory did not include fermions was a death sentence if it could not be fixed.

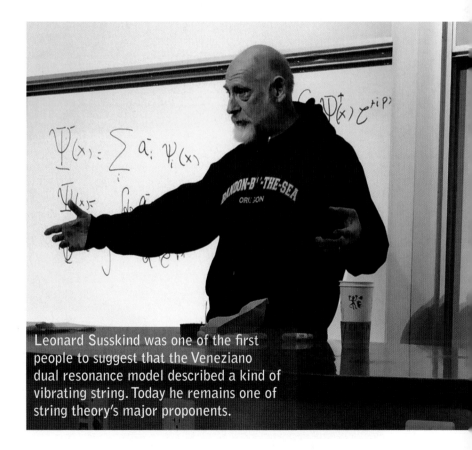

Leonard Susskind was one of the first people to suggest that the Veneziano dual resonance model described a kind of vibrating string. Today he remains one of string theory's major proponents.

Rejection and Acceptance in String Theory

The first time Leonard Susskind tried to submit his paper describing the dual resonance model as a theory of strings, he got this note back: "This paper is not terribly important, and it doesn't predict any new experimental results, and I don't think it's publishable in the *Physical Review*." Though crushed, Susskind did find another journal that accepted his paper shortly after that.

A few years after this first paper Susskind would attend a lecture by Murray Gell-Mann, a Nobel-winning particle physicist. After the lecture Gell-Man asked what Susskind studied while they rode an elevator together. He said, "I'm working on this theory that [particles] are like rubber bands, these one-dimensional stringy things." At which point Gell-Mann laughed at him. Two years later Gell-Mann would approach Susskind again and apologize for his laughter. Susskind recounted what Gell-Mann said:

> The stuff you're doing is the greatest stuff in the world. It's just absolutely fantastic, and in my concluding talk at the conference I'm going to talk about nothing but your stuff. We've got to sit down during the conference and talk about it. You've got to explain it to me carefully, so that I get it right.

SUPERSTRING THEORY

Pierre Ramond (1943–), a French physicist working in America, was determined to find a way to make the mathematics work for bosonic string theory. He went about figuring out how to create a version of string theory that included both bosons and fermions. Starting in 1971 and spurred on by the work of Nambu, Nielsen, and Susskind, he found that by adding supersymmetry to string theory you could find more of the particles we see in our universe.

Supersymmetry is the idea that for every type of force particle (like a photon) there would be a matching mass particle (like an electron). By adding supersymmetry to bosonic string theory, Ramond advanced the field leaps and bounds. This added fermions to the theory, but supersymmetry also lowered the required number of dimensions to a mere ten. When people talk about string theory today they almost always mean supersymmetric string theory or superstring theory. From here on out, when we refer to string theory we mean superstring theory. Ramond's work in supersymmetry would also inspire the next two important string theorists.

STRING THEORY AS A THEORY of GRAVITY

In 1974, two scientists would make history. Joël Scherk (1946–1979) and John Schwarz (1941–) worked together on string theory, and their work changed the field once again. Scherk came to the United States to study from his native France. He was assigned Schwarz, a young professor, as a mentor at Princeton. Schwarz found himself devoting his career to string theory and solving its mysteries. For this reason he will be mentioned several more times during his collaboration with other string theorists. At this point in time many of Schwarz's and Scherk's peers had abandoned string

John Schwarz, currently the Harold Brown Professor of Theoretical Physics at the California Institute of Technology, is one of the people behind the first superstring revolution.

theory for more promising research because they felt that the mathematics were hinting at something much deeper. Both of them were compelled to follow these equations to see where they would lead.

Together Scherk and Schwarz realized that one of the particles required by string theory could actually be a graviton. A graviton is what physicists believe is the quantum particle responsible for the gravity we see on larger scales. This made them the first people to suggest string theory as a theory of quantum gravity.

The fact that Scherk and Schwarz found a potential graviton in the theory was important news. Rather than everyone else's work that involved trying to fit a square gravity particle in a round quantum physics hole, string theory already had gravity in it. But in spite of how exciting this was, there were still too many problems in the mathematics. These problems, called anomalies, kept many physicists from working on string theory, and the discovery made by Scherk and Schwarz went relatively unnoticed.

As a result of superstring theory, Scherk and two new collaborators, Ferdinando Gliozzi (1940–) and David Olive (1937–2012), found that superstring theory did not have another troublesome particle bosonic string theory originally predicted. Beside the lack of fermions like electrons, another problem bosonic string theory had was an impossible predicted particle.

Many theories predict new particles, but they should not predict particles we know to be impossible. This predicted particle, called a tachyon, had a speed faster than light. As we know from Einstein's first work with relativity, there is nothing that can go faster than the speed of light. Thanks to supersymmetry the troublesome tachyon was removed from the theory. The work that Scherk, Gliozzi, and Olive did helped prove to some of their colleagues that superstring theory was on the right track. Eva Silverstein, another prominent string theorist, expanded on the mathematics of Sherk, Gliozzi, and Olive to further disprove the existence of a tachyon in superstring theory. String theory still was not a hugely popular field to work in. Thanks to these few pioneers, though, it was looking better and better for being the theory of quantum gravity and the theory of everything.

The FIRST SUPERSTRING REVOLUTION

In 1979 Schwarz began working with Michael Green, a British physicist. This collaboration would change the history of string theory. The two first met at CERN, the same institution that Veneziano worked at when he published his dual resonance model. Working together for the better part of five years, in 1984 they finally managed to remove all anomalies from the equations of string theory. In physics and mathematics, anomalies are the deadly enemy of successful theories. That these two scientists were able to solve the anomalies meant string theory was a fresh and viable solution to quantum gravity. It required nine dimensions, plus one of time, but this seemed tame to the twenty-six dimensions originally called for in bosonic string theory. This is how Schwarz and Green started the first superstring revolution. Schwarz described string theory's meteoric rise to popularity as going from "an intellectual backwater to the mainstream of theoretical physics." The work that Schwarz and Green dedicated themselves to caused an explosion of research and new ideas.

One of the first big discoveries to come out of the first superstring revolution that Schwarz and Green began was heterotic string theory. The people behind it were a group of four mathematicians and theoretical physicists. They are often referred to as the Princeton String Quartet by their colleagues (to give you an idea of a mathematician's sense of humor). Together David Gross, Jeffrey Harvey, Emil Martinec, and Ryan Rohm presented their idea in 1985. Though the mathematics are mind-numbingly complicated, the end result is they were able to make the world of string theory simpler. The Princeton String Quartet helped explain the way the extra dimensions the theory called for worked in reality.

In the next ten years hundreds of people would work on string theory. You would think this was a good thing, but it spelled trouble. The more people working on string theory, the more versions of the theory there came to be, and the theories seemed extremely different on the surface. Scientists did not understand how string theory could be right if it could make such different variations. And if it was right, which of these versions actually explained our universe?

M-THEORY and the SECOND SUPERSTRING REVOLUTION

It took ten years and one of the greatest minds of our time, a man named Ed Witten (1951–), to resolve this issue. Ed Witten's father was a theoretical physicist himself. Together they were talking about physics by the time Witten was four. Witten was brilliant enough to go into almost any field he wanted. Initially he studied history and linguistics in college, but several years later he returned to study at Princeton to get a degree in mathematics. He switched partway through and studied physics instead. He happened to have one of the members of the Princeton String Quartet, David Gross, as his graduate advisor. Many believe Witten's basis in mathematics gives him an unrivaled understanding of theoretical physics. It was his research on the different versions of string theory that made him one of the most important figures in string theory. Through his research he realized all of the different string theories were linked intricately and deeply within their mathematics.

In 1994 Witten would tell the world what he had discovered in his research. He gave a game-changing talk at the annual string theory meeting. Witten single-handedly started the second string theory revolution with this talk. He revealed that all the versions of string theory were united in their mathematics. Imagine each of the versions of string theory as different squares. Witten was the one to realize that all of the squares could be joined together to form a cube. This allowed string theory to form a new, more complete view of the universe. He called this new group string theory equation M-theory. The "m" he explained, could stand for whatever you wanted: mystery, magic, or membrane. Witten felt uncomfortable naming something that he could not fully explain and decided to leave it up to others as more work was completed.

As a result of Witten's M-theory hypothesis, many people began looking at a new object in string theory called a brane.

Ed Witten is the mind behind the realization of M-theory. Today Witten teaches mathematical physics at the Institute for Advanced Study in Princeton, New Jersey, the same institution Albert Einstein taught at when he immigrated to the United States.

A brane is a multidimensional object. The most familiar brane is one that occurs in two dimensions, or a membrane. But branes can get very complicated quickly (they have up to nine dimensions) and have novel properties in the theory itself. In 1995 Joseph Polchinski, a professor at University of California Santa Barbara, proposed that strings themselves could end on D-branes. This allowed for even more possibilities for open strings and created many new research pathways.

STRING THEORY and PUBLIC EDUCATION

It is hard to talk about important people in string theory without talking about the scientists that have made it accessible to people across the world. Brian Greene, Michio Kaku, and Neil deGrasse Tyson have all been huge figures in the public's mind when it comes to string theory and theoretical physics. Through popular science lectures, books, and television specials, these scientists (and others) have allowed the public to access the weird and wonderful world of string theory. Without them it is likely this book would not have happened.

By energizing the public to think about theoretical physics these men have made a huge contribution to the field. Without the public's excitement, funding for new experiments and places for theoretical physicists to work would be unlikely to exist. Because string theory is a long way off from practical applications it means that funding for research can be much more difficult to get. Together Green, Kaku, deGrasse Tyson, and others have made the world excited to see what comes next in this developing field.

String theory is like a trail of breadcrumbs. For the last sixty years, every time one physicist has made a breakthrough, we have followed that person's work to the next person he or she inspired. From Euler to Witten, string theory is populated by some of the most brilliant and revolutionary minds of the last three hundred years. In addition, each great string theorist has helped advise new string theorists. With this great set of minds in the world today there is no telling where string theory will go next.

This is an artist's rendering of what the subatomic world looks like according to string theory on a very small scale. These vibrating strands of energy allow the randomness of quantum physics to coexist with the smooth fabric of space-time that general relativity and gravity require.

CHAPTER 4

The Discovery of String Theory

When talking about string theory there are lots of versions one could discuss. String theory is interesting because of its unique ideas about the universe and the weird scenarios it presents. It offers an unusual way to think about our universe and the matter within it. On the other hand, it has proved almost impossible to directly test so far. The mathematics are so complicated scientists have not yet been able to solve for the equation that describes our universe. In spite of this, it remains one of the best options for a theory of quantum gravity and a theory of everything.

WHAT IS STRING THEORY?

At its heart, string theory is about strings. There are other things that make string theory unusual as well. String theory's main idea is that all of the subatomic particles in quantum physics are actually made of much smaller vibrating strands of energy. The strings can vibrate from left to right, or right to left, and the different ways they vibrate determines the kind of particle they create.

After John Schwarz and Michael Green's work in 1984, there was an explosion of researchers working on string theory.

This lead to the first superstring revolution. The more people worked on string theory, the more versions of it there became. It was confusing to scientists. If string theory were really correct then how could there be five versions that seemed so different?

By the end of the first superstring revolution there were five versions of string theory. They include type I, type IIA, type IIB, HE, and HO. For the purposes of this book all one needs to understand about symmetry is that O(32) and E_8xE_8 symmetry groups are mathematically different ways of expressing symmetry. Type I has symmetry group O(32) and involves open and closed strings. Type IIA has closed strings with symmetrical vibration patterns no matter which way the vibrations are traveling. The other special thing about Type IIA is that the open strings are connected to special structures called D-branes, which become important in later versions of string theory. Type IIB is very similar to IIA, but the closed strings have asymmetrical vibrations depending on whether the vibrations move left or right. The other versions of string theory, HO and HE, are named after heterotic strings. In heterotic strings the different directions of the vibrations, left or right, resulted in different particles. The main difference between HE and HO string theories is the form of symmetry they use. HO uses the O(32) group symmetry, and HE uses the E_8xE_8 group symmetry. All of these versions of string theory have nine dimensions of space and one of time.

M-Theory

M-theory was developed in 1995 by Ed Witten as a way of joining all of the differing versions of string theory that were developed in the first superstring revolution. Witten and other physicists working on string theory discovered there were certain dualities in the mathematics. A duality is when there are two distinctly different ways to look at the same event or phenomenon.

In all the versions of string theory there were two types of duality. T-duality refers to the topological duality, where there are two ways of explaining the same space. S-duality refers to the strong-weak duality, where the strong force of one theory can be equated to the weak force of another. Realizing these dualities hinted at a deeper connection between all the versions of string theory, Witten began creating M-theory.

In M-theory, the "M" can stand for "mystery," "magic," or "membrane." At the time, Witten felt that he could not explain the theory well enough to confidently name it. He called it M-theory with the hope that some day it would be understood well enough for someone else to come up with a more comprehensive name.

Gravity and Quantum Mechanics

One of the major developments of string theory is that it is a theory of how gravity works on the scale of particles. This is important because string theory was found to inherently include gravity. It surprised the scientists working on string theory as well because they did not set out to create a theory of gravity.

The reason string theory works as a theory of gravity is that particle interactions happen over the length of strings and in the area of branes. In the Standard Model view of the world, particles are finite points. Their interactions are all based on the probability a subatomic particle will do a certain thing. Because the interactions for point-based particles (like those of the Standard Model) require that the particles touch to interact, the distance between the particles is zero, and the interaction happens at a single point in space time. The equations for gravitons and gravity fall apart at zero distance and a single point of space. Gravity in the Standard Model produces nonsense answers because of this. But in string theory the interaction between particles happens over the length of the strings. This allows for the equations to make reasonable answers. Gravity and gravitons work with the mathematics of a string-based particle.

Gravity is a hard force to explain on the scale of the very small. Most of the equations that need gravity are on the scale of planets and stars. Because the other three forces are stronger but are only effective on a much smaller distance (like the diameter of a proton or atom) they have no effect on stars. When scientists seek to explain how something as massive as a star but as small as a quantum particle works, they need a unified theory of all four forces. Black holes and the beginning of the universe (the big bang and even before) are a fascinating area of research that require a theory of quantum gravity. String theory may be just the thing to give researchers new insights and potential answers to these questions.

HOW DOES STRING THEORY WORK?

There are a few key things to know about how string theory works. There are strings, extra dimensions, super symmetry, and membranes. Today when people discuss string theory, they often refer to the most current version of the string theory, M-theory. The mathematics behind M-theory are extremely complicated. Witten's intimate understanding of the mathematics and their consequences make him one of the few people able to create and realize M-theory.

The new string theory, M-theory, has some new concepts and some familiar string theory concepts. Like other versions of string theory, it involves strings, multiple dimensions, and supersymmetry. The most novel additions of M-theory were branes and an extra dimension of space. All the previous versions of string theory coming out of the first superstring revolution had ten total dimensions. M-theory added yet another dimension, bringing the total to eleven. Physicists were willing to accept another dimension, however, because it once again united string theory.

Strings

The strings in string theory are incredibly small, vibrating strands of energy. If strings exist, they are about 10^{-33} of a centimeter long. If you imagine an atom as the size of planet Earth, the length of one of the strings making up the particles in the atom would be about a yard long. One of the things that makes string theory very difficult to confirm or disprove is how tiny the strings are. Currently we have no technology capable of detecting them because it would require so much energy.

It is also important that the strings vibrate. Without vibrations string theory would not be able to explain the great diversity we see in particles. In stringed instruments, like the guitar, the string vibrates to create a noise we hear. Depending on how the guitar string vibrates, the note the guitar makes will change. In this way one string on the guitar can make a whole range of notes by changing nothing but its vibrations. The same is true for string theory. The different vibrations of the strings in string theory create the different particles seen in quantum physics.

Strings can be open or closed in M-theory. Closed strings have the option of vibrating left or right around the string. This affects what particle the string appears as. Open strings can interact with other strings and branes creating different results. On the scale scientists can observe, they would see a particle interaction that normally would be described by ordinary quantum physics.

There are five fundamental interactions strings can undergo. All these changes involve joining or splitting the string to make a new configuration. A single string can join its two endpoints to form a closed string. An open string can also bud off some of its length to result in a closed string and

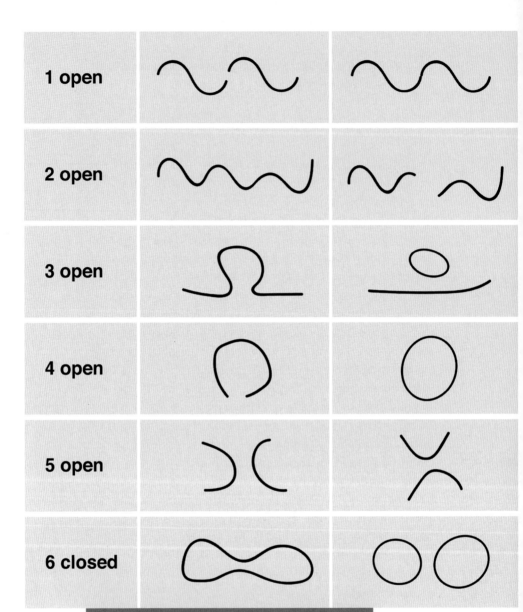

1 open		
2 open		
3 open		
4 open		
5 open		
6 closed		

This figure details the six basic interactions open and closed strings can have. The open strings' ends attach to membranes, or branes, and its ends can join other strings or itself.

open string. An open string can split into two open strings. Two open strings can switch with each other the brane they attach to. Finally one closed string can split to form two closed strings. All of these strings will have different vibrations as they interact. When particles break down or in some way change in the Standard Model, it can be viewed as their vibrations and/ or configuration changing in the string theory model. Through their different vibrations, strings make all the subatomic particles we see in the quantum physics model.

Extra Dimensions

Perhaps one of the most difficult things to understand about string theory is the fact that it calls for many dimensions. Extra dimensions are one of the strangest features of M-theory. We live on a four-dimensional plane. We have three spatial dimensions (length, width, height) and one dimension of time. String theory, in contrast, requires eleven dimensions. This is so foreign to us it takes a little work to understand how it could be possible.

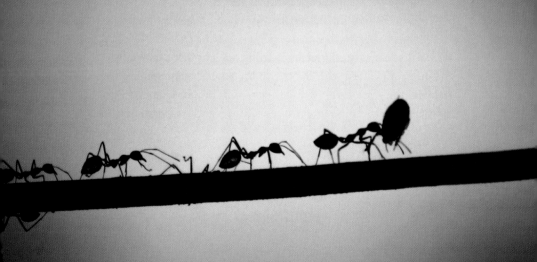

On our scale, it seems like a wire has only one dimension— length. But to the ants walking on the same wire, it has two dimensions—length and width.

When we look at a telephone wire from far away, it seems like it has one dimension, length. But to an ant on that telephone wire, the wire has length and width. Think about the wire as a cylinder on the ant's scale. The cylinder is a rolled rectangle, giving it width and length. In this way, something that seems like it has one dimension on our scale could have two dimensions to an observer on a smaller scale. If we took that same telephone wire and tied it into a knot, we would be able to allow for even more dimensions. Mathematical hiding of dimensions like this is called compactification. Compactification is one way to explain the extra dimensions of string theory and why we only experience a few dimensions on our scale.

The other option to explain all the dimensions we cannot experience is that we are stuck on a three-dimensional plane. Imagine a square and a circle stuck on a piece of paper. For the square and the circle, trying to understand the way a cube or sphere works would be very difficult. The sphere itself could not exist in only two dimensions because it would simply be a circle. These dimensions are outside of our plane (or brane, as string theorists would say) in the same way as the sphere and are inaccessible to scientists.

Membranes

Associated with the multiple dimensions, one of the newer additions to string theory is the idea of membranes, called "branes." When Ed Witten first unveiled his new unified theory of the previous five versions of string theory it required an extra dimension. Think back to that example of compactification with the telephone wire. Witten realized that an eleven-dimension string theory with branes wrapped into strings looked the same as a ten-dimension string theory with only strings.

Branes can have two dimensions, called 2-branes, creating something like a piece of fabric. Branes can have up to nine dimensions! This makes them very hard to visualize or understand using anything scientists experience in our three-dimensional world. The interesting thing about branes is that they may be one of the best ways to explain what happens at the edge of a black hole. Physicists realized that branes are very sticky and grab onto objects around them, just like the edge of a black hole grabs onto objects.

The branes of string theory can have many dimensions, but they have other characteristics as well. Branes can also have charge, so they interact with each other and other particles through something similar to the electromagnetic force. Branes have a unique characteristic called tension. In a trampoline

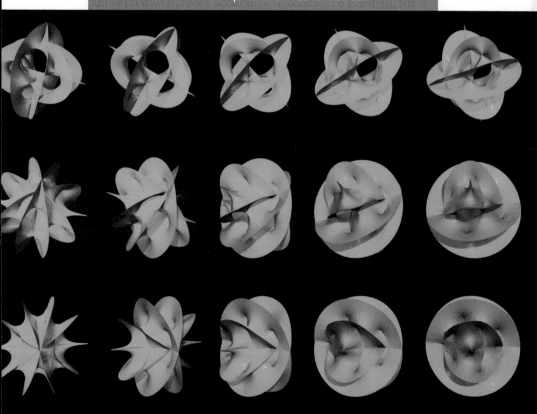

Using a computer model, string theorists have started to imagine what these multidimensional strings and branes look like. These complicated-looking shapes reflect even more complicated mathematics.

there is not so much tension that the surface will not give under your weight. But a trampoline has to have some tension or you would sink to the ground without bouncing back up.

Tension in branes is like a trampoline. A trampoline or brane with infinite tension would be so hard that someone jumping on it would smack into it like concrete and never bounce back. Likewise, someone jumping on a trampoline or brane with zero tension would sink to the ground and never bounce back. Tension in branes is a measure of how easily the brane is influenced by interactions with other particles. If a brane has zero tension it is completely deformed by an interaction. If it has infinite tension no other particle will change it.

While branes were hypothesized right after the first superstring revolution, it was not until M-theory that they became an integral part. They were necessary to unite all the different versions of string theory.

Supersymmetry

Supersymmetry was first introduced into string theory in 1981 by Michael Green and John Schwarz. Every version of string theory has had supersymmetry since then. This is required by the mathematics. Without supersymmetry certain parts of the equations cannot be cancelled out and there are anomalies in the mathematics. So supersymmetry is another necessary condition of string theory. The "super" refers to the fact that every particle we see in the Standard Model has a partner. This means that the eighteen particles predicted by the Standard Model become thirty-six in string theory. This is a lot of particles! The superpartners of the bosons end with "ino." So the superpartner of the gluon is the gluino and of the photon is the photino, and so on. The superpartners of the fermions begin with "s," so there are selectrons, squarks, and sneutrinos to name a few.

These superpartners may only have existed at the energy levels in the nanoseconds following the big bang. This means we may never see these particles in any experiment we can perform because it is likely they require too much energy. It is important to note that even if string theory is disproven, many scientists believe it is possible that supersymmetry may be correct. There are several other theories of quantum physics that require supersymmetry as well, so this is not a unique feature of string theory.

TESTING STRING THEORY

Disproving string theory is harder than it sounds because absence of proof is not the same as proof of absence. The absence of proof for the Loch Ness monster (however improbable) is not the same as proof the Loch Ness monster does not exist. This may sound crazy to say, but it is a tenet of the scientific method. One of the problems with string theory, outside of the extremely complicated mathematics, is that the size of the strings is so small that there is no way to directly observe them. In the scientific method, a scientist comes up with a hypothesis, tests the hypothesis using experimentation, and then makes new hypotheses from the results of the experiments. But string theory denies this ability to make hypotheses and to test them.

Part of the problem is string theory is incomplete. Even M-theory is not finished yet. The reason for this is the mathematics have many possible answers. Finding the right string theory and its exact numbers that describe our universe may take years, if not decades. From current calculations there are about 10^{500} viable string theories. That's a one followed by five hundred zeroes, so this number is enormously large, but not infinite. These are theories where the numbers work out to be complete and make sense. The problem now is finding

This photograph of Blue Gene, an IBM super computer, shows the massive power of many hundreds of processors linked together. These supercomputers are involved in solving equations in string theory.

the needle in the 10^{500} haystacks. The search continues for the exact, complete theory that explains our universe.

Another problem is that because string theory is incomplete, there are currently no unique predictions that can be tested. String theory is very good at coming up with mathematical explanations for the data we already have. It struggles to come up with unique predictions that can be tested. When Einstein proposed his radical idea of general relativity it made unique predictions. For instance, general relativity predicted that light would be affected by gravity. During the 1919 solar eclipse scientists were able to see stars that were directly behind the sun. The gravitational effect on light Einstein predicted was actually observed.

But string theory currently does not have a testable prediction like gravitational lensing. Most string theorists feel that the best option for testing string theory is black holes. String theory did not set out to create an explanation for black holes. The p-branes, a special type of brane, are a result of the mathematics of string theory. The fact that they line up very well

Supercomputers Advance String Theory

A supercomputer is one of the most powerful tools string theorists today have. In general a supercomputer is a computer at the highest level of computational capacity. This means it can do mathematics faster than any human being alive by a huge margin. Supercomputers are capable of handling the incredibly complex mathematics required by string theory's equations. This makes them important to string theorists as they search for the "correct" version of string theory that describes our universe.

Many of the rapid advances in string theory in the last two decades have been due in part to modern supercomputers. Supercomputers can potentially help us find the numbers required for the version of string theory that correctly describes our universe. Scientists and mathematicians often use "modeling" to help see what the equations they have predict should happen. By comparing the differences between the modeled world and the actual world, scientists gain insight into their ideas and where reality is different. A great example of this is trying to find out what the universe was like right after the big bang. By using a supercomputer to do the mathematical modeling, we get new ideas about how string theory may or may not work.

The results of a particle collision at the Large Hadron Collider look something like this. Each of these lines and dots and spirals resulting from the collision of hadron particles shows the tiny subatomic particles making up the world around us.

with how we think black holes may work is a coincidence, but an important one. The connection between the way p-branes and black holes work is seen as a major step toward potential evidence supporting string theory. The mathematics, some string theorists feel, are too perfect to be mere coincidence.

Looking at Gravity

More evidence for string theory (and potential ways to test it) may be found from gravity outside of our three dimensions. There are two ways to test this. One is to look on the very small scale to see if there is a violation of the inverse-square law that we know to be true for gravity. This would show that gravity itself behaves differently on the scale of subatomic particles and atoms. Another theory involves the compactification of dimensions that string theorists use. If this compactification is correct, then gravity may behave differently in the compactified dimensions. To look at both of these, scientists are using experiments at particle accelerators like the Large Hadron Collider.

Brane Worlds

One potentially testable idea is that we may be living within a brane. In exploring branes, some physicists came to believe that our own three-dimensional existence (excluding time) is the result of us living on a 3-brane. There is a fundamental difference between our 3-brane world dimensions and the dimensions off of and outside of the 3-brane.

This is an interesting idea because it would help explain why we cannot experience or potentially ever find the other dimensions in our experiments. It may be that gravity and dimensions are entirely different outside of the 3-brane we are within. If scientists can see the extra dimensions behaving differently than our own, it may be evidence for string theory and the idea of a brane world.

Holographic Principle

The holographic principle relates to the surface of an object (like a brane) holding the information of the objects within it. A holograph is a two-dimensional image containing all the information of the three-dimensional object it represents. Every object contains information. You contain information about the exact arrangement of all the atoms and particles that make you. The holographic principle says that all the information about the particles within something (no matter how large) is contained on the surface of the region they exist within. If one were standing within a cube, the holographic principle says that each side of the cube would contain the two-dimensional information about oneself. This is surprising because at first scientists believed that in order to completely recreate something three-dimensional they would need three dimensions worth of information. But the holographic principle says just by looking at the surface of one's cube, someone would know all the three-dimensional information about oneself. Another result of the holographic principle is the idea our four-dimensional world (with time) is actually the holograph on the edge of a 5-brane. The possibilities of the holographic principle are a little mind-bending to say the least.

The holographic principle may be useful in understanding how black holes work. Physicists first studying general relativity made a startling discovery. If an object was massive enough, the distortion it would make in space-time would be so steep that past a certain point, not even light would be able to escape it. They called it a black hole because of this. There is also a point of no return surrounding the black hole called the event horizon. Once something is past the event horizon it cannot escape the black hole no matter what. This leads scientists to wonder what happens to the information that describes the objects that disappear into a black hole. The holographic principle says that the information from these objects is preserved on the very edge of the black hole as a kind of hologram. Physicists, cosmologists, and string theorists are hoping to study more black holes and look at the data from them. If the information of the objects that is contained within them is stored somehow on the event horizon, this may be evidence for the holographic principle and string theory.

Supersymmetry

Another way to potentially test string theory would be to look for supersymmetry. If supersymmetry can be disproven, then string theory would be disproven. But remember, the energy levels that the supersymmetrical partners exist at is so high that they may have only existed right after the big bang. It is entirely possible that we will not be able to create an experiment using the available equipment that would be able to reach the energy levels needed to observe particles like gluinos, photinos, and selectrons. If supersymmetry is proven to exist then it would be one more piece of evidence in support of string theory. However, even if supersymmetry is proven to exist, string theory still may not be correct because there are other theories that use supersymmetry as well.

Scientists are not sure why superpartners have not yet been observed because it seems like there have been collisions of high enough energy to see them. It is possible that the superpartners are so heavy that even if they have been created in these collisions they degrade faster than we can record them. Dark matter provides another opportunity for string theory to test its mettle. Dark matter is matter that gives off little to no detectable radiation in the universe. This makes it almost impossible to detect from planet Earth. But the equations show that there is some form of matter we have not observed making up the universe. The gravitational forces scientists observe in the universe are higher than they should be with only the visible matter they detect. This is where dark matter comes in. It explains this unseen matter affecting gravity in the universe. Some string theorists propose that the dark matter of the universe is really made of superpartners from supersymmetry, like the photino. If dark matter is found to be composed of supersymmetry partners it would be a big step forward in support of string theory and supersymmetry.

The CONTROVERSY of STRING THEORY

Many string theorists acknowledge the need for more theories to be developed. One of the largest dangers of a popular idea like string theory is that there will be no opposing theories that can be tested against it. Even worse is the danger of "groupthink." Psychologists have shown that if you put people who think the same way at the same table, the conversation is meaningless because they will always agree with one another. By developing opposing theories of quantum gravity and potential theories of everything, scientists can compare and contrast. This meeting of the minds and critical thinking help advance science more than anything else.

Opponents of string theory argue that because it cannot be tested, string theory is not really a scientific theory. At best it is a philosophy because it is something that can never be shown to be disproven scientifically. One of the things that has allowed string theory to last so long is its ability to adapt and change to suit new mathematics and ideas. This same adaptability is string theory's weakness. It can adapt to any new piece of evidence that might seem to disprove it. Critics say this apparently limitless diversity means it is impossible to reject the hypothesis it makes, therefore it is not a scientific theory.

There is some support for a theory with elegant mathematics that is difficult to experimentally prove. The Higgs boson was proposed as a way for molecules to gain mass. Without the Higgs boson, how particles had mass was nearly impossible to explain on a quantum level. The Higgs-less mathematics were downright ugly and convoluted. This led researchers to believe even if they could not prove that the Higgs boson existed, it was highly likely that it did. The mathematics were there in support of it. It took forty years and the construction of the largest particle accelerator in the world (the Large Hadron Collider) to finally find experimental evidence of the Higgs boson. The elegant mathematics of string theory are very reminiscent of the Higgs boson problem. It is one of the reasons that in spite of all the struggles and challenges string theory poses, physicists continue to work on it.

String theory's best hope is that it stands the test of time and everything thrown against it. Whether or not the experiments come back confirming things like supersymmetry or the holographic principle on the edge of black holes remains to be seen.

The THEORY of EVERYTHING

One reason people continue to work on string theory is because of the ultimate goal of understanding gravity on a quantum scale and being able to unify all four forces in a single theory. Whether or not string theory will be proven true is not clear. There are several experiments that may prove existence of a possible side effect of the theory but direct proof is a long way off.

Today's physicists are carrying on with Einstein's final quest of a unified theory of everything. This is the holy grail of modern physics. While the Standard Model can explain three forces, it cannot explain gravity. Gravity and quantum physics are fatally incompatible using the current scientific models. String theorists believe that they may have the answer to a unified theory of everything with string theory.

Unification of the four physical forces is one of the goals of string theory. In one sense unification is about creating a single theory that allows for all of the physical forces. But on a deeper

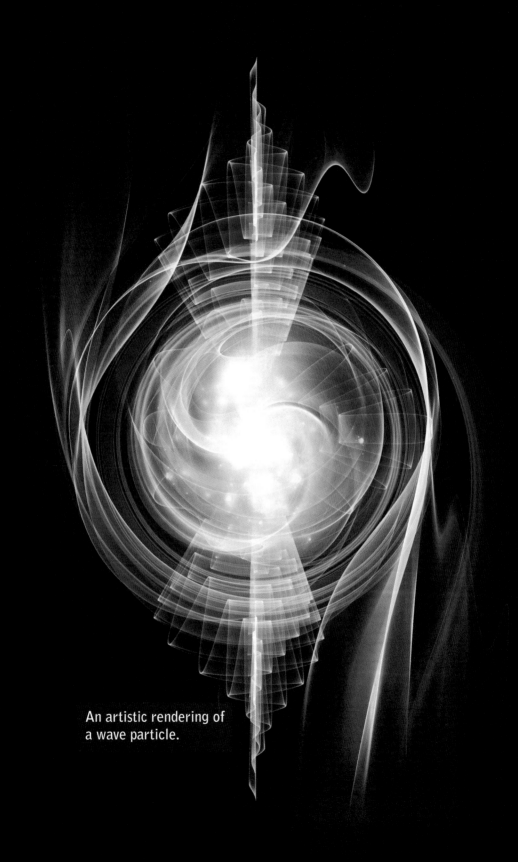
An artistic rendering of
a wave particle.

sense, physicists believe that in the milliseconds after the big bang, it is possible that all four forces were actually one force.

This is not the first time someone has suggested the forces could be unified. Physicists working on the Standard Model discovered something similar. At very high energy levels, like those right after the big bang, the electromagnetic force and the weak force are actually the same. This electroweak force leads physicists to think it may be possible that all four forces were once the same force at even higher energy levels. But because our universe now exists at a much lower energy level the forces appear different.

So far there are not many other contenders for a theory of united forces and quantum gravity. No one has yet been able to make a version of the Standard Model that allows for gravity. Some scientists have proposed that it is possible we may need to rethink the theory of general relativity itself to try and make sense of it on a quantum scale. Because of the different ways that strings interact in string theory, it allows for gravity on a small scale. Many other theories do not allow for this. One option is loop quantum gravity, which we will discuss more in the next chapter. In spite of the complex mathematics and challenges presented by experiments to test it, string theory has prevailed. It remains one of the best options for the theory of quantum gravity and a general theory of everything.

The search for a unified field theory is the search to unite the realms of the cosmos and subatomic at last. So far string theory is one of the main contenders in this quest.

String Theory Today

String theory has had a large influence on both the public's mind and the next generation of physicists. While it is controversial for its lack of predictions, it continues to enthrall the minds of many with its bizarre conditions and conclusions. It is yet to be seen how history will see string theory: as a misstep like luminiferous ether or a brilliant idea like general relativity and quantum mechanics.

One thing is for sure: love it or hate it, string theory catches the imaginations of physicists and the public alike. Brian Greene and Michio Kaku, two prominent string theorists, have both done a lot of public education and made the strange mathematics of string theory available to a wide audience. String theory has a lot of strange properties that make it intriguing and compelling. At this point, it is a question of whether string theory and its mathematics will live up to the hype.

RELEVANCY of STRING THEORY

String theorists would say string theory will always be relevant. But has string theory been overhyped? Or unfairly criticized? So far it has withstood changes due to discoveries in the field and adapted to everything critics have thrown at it. Critics are

Physicist Brian Greene has been key in expanding support and communicating the science of string theory. With his books and TV specials he has made theoretical physics exciting and engaging for the public.

not so sure of its relevancy. Until scientists can determine more ways to test it, it may not be relevant.

The relevancy of string theory can also be measured in the toolkit it provides to look at the universe. Amanda Peet, a famous string theorist working on black holes, describes them like building blocks. From concepts like strings and branes there are a huge number of different ways to assemble things like black holes and the big bang.

For better or worse, one thing keeping string theory relevant and at the forefront of theoretical physics is its versatility. As new discoveries are made (like the expansion of the universe) equations can be adapted to incorporate these results. You might say what string theorists say—that string theory can be made to fit the results so it is still right. But this versatility can be problematic as well. Because it has proven so adaptable, it will be very difficult to disprove it outright.

Quantum Gravity but not Quantum General Relativity

It remains that string theory is one of the only viable theories of quantum gravity. The only real challenger is loop quantum gravity, which we will discuss later in this chapter. One major problem with most current versions of string theory is that they are background-dependent theories. This means the space-time background of string theory is fixed.

Critics point out that because of this, string theory really is not a theory of quantum general relativity. If it is not a theory of general relativity, then how could it really unite the four forces and become a theory of everything? General relativity requires the fabric of space-time to be dynamic or changeable. But this is not a problem unique to string theory, as the standard model and many other quantum field theories are background dependent. One option for making string theory background independent is actually incorporating some of the ideas from loop quantum gravity, the main opposing theory of quantum gravity.

The Right Equation

One of the great determining factors of string theory and its relevancy today to science will be whether or not the right set of numbers to plug into these equations can be found. If scientists can narrow down string theory to find the right set of numbers that describes our universe, many of its troubles will be solved. Unfortunately this is a big if. At this point, it may be too much of a long shot. As we discussed in the last chapter, the current options for viable string theories are 10^{500}. This number is incomprehensibly large, and many have given up hope of ever finding the string theory that describes our universe. String theory is a lot like a puzzle. Physicists have billions and billions of pieces that they can assemble together to create the picture, but they have to assemble all the pieces together in the right way to create the picture of our universe. The equations work with many numbers, but finding the numbers that match up to what we see in the world is going to be the ultimate challenge. If there is a third string theory revolution, this may be the thing that spurs it on.

Critics of string theory say this number means it is likely that string theory will never describe our exact universe. Without knowing the correct equation, string theorists also have a very hard time coming up with testable predictions. Many great minds of string theory, like Leonard Susskind and Ed Witten, have turned to the anthropic principle for lack of hope about finding the "right" string theory to describe our own universe. Critics view this as a cop out, taking the easy path.

The Anthropic Principle

In 2003 Susskind introduced the idea of a "string theory" landscape. This relies on the anthropic principle, which is controversial for many scientists. The anthropic principle states that the universe behaves the way it does because we are here to observe it. This same principle is often used to lend support to the existence of a supernatural creator or architect. To use the anthropic principle as a way of redefining string theory's goals is nothing short of scandalous for some scientists.

Susskind, however, invokes it in a different fashion. We can only observe the portions of the universe in which the laws allow us to exist. Imagine that for each of the supposed answers to string theory there is a universe that they explain. This means that our universe is one of many, a part of the multiverse. If there were only one universe then we would have to explain how conditions came to be perfect to allow for our existence. But in an almost limitless series of random universes a universe that allows for observers like us to exist is bound to happen by sheer chance.

The anthropic principle is seen by many as a cop-out. Critics view this as failure to answer the question of how string theory in our universe works by changing the question to how string theory in all universes works. At best it is a rationalization for the fact that no single string theory has been found to describe our exact universe yet. At worst the anthropic principle is revisionary history trying to remake the quest of string theory into one of exploration, not answer-seeking. In spite of this, the anthropic principle is gaining begrudging support. Ed Witten, the father of M-theory, has turned to it due to lack of other options. There may not be a single theory at the end of the multiverse. If this is the case, some argue string theory may be too vast to explain anything.

The anthropic principle is still highly contentious for many scientists. But if true, for every possible string theory that exists, there is a corresponding universe. Together these possible universes would form the "string theory landscape," as physicist Leonard Susskind has dubbed it.

Testing String Theory

As string theorists come up with more ways for string theory to be tested, it becomes more and more likely that the theory will have more answers. So far there have been no direct tests proposed because the strings are too small to observe using any of our technology.

If scientists can find ways to test string theory, like looking for supersymmetry or extra dimensions, this may help make it more relevant. However, there are other theories that call for extra dimensions and supersymmetry. This means that even if extra dimensions or supersymmetry are shown to exist it would be support for string theory but not direct proof. Finding direct evidence of the vibrating strings, though currently impossible, might be the only way string theory has to win over the hearts and minds of its critics.

ADVANCES FROM STRING THEORY

String theory has helped several areas of science. Because of the math required, there have been several advances in the world of pure mathematics. It has also allowed scientists to make advances in how we think about the universe we live in. Many string theorists believe that even if the theory is disproven, parts of string theory will continue to be important in modern physics. Examples of this are holograms, extra dimensions, and supersymmetry. One of the most promising areas that string theory has made advances in is the study of black holes.

Pure Mathematics

In the field of pure mathematics, string theory is a goldmine. Pure mathematics has advanced because of the unusual forms and the complicated equations of string theory. These have lead to several breakthroughs, like the Calabi-Yau manifolds. The

Criticism of String Theory

String theory critics argue that the theory is not relevant any more. According to its critics, string theory cannot be falsified or proven wrong and it does not make any unique, testable predictions. The words "unique" and "testable" are both hugely important. String theory does predict extra dimensions and supersymmetry, but neither of these predictions is unique. Other theories require them as well. So even if supersymmetry or extra dimensions are discovered, there are other theories that they could relate to instead of string theory. In terms of testability, this is even more important. The one idea completely unique to string theory is the strings it is named after. Unfortunately, they are so small that scientists doubt they will ever be able to find a way to directly observe them.

A theory that makes no predictions has no scientific purpose, critics argue. Some have argued that string theory is a philosophy, or at best a branch of higher mathematics. Critics also point out that in spite of the problems facing string theory it still receives the majority of available funding. This has lead, some say, to a lack of opposing theories because there is no money to develop or research alternatives to string theory.

Calabi-Yau manifolds are in part responsible for how string theorists view compactified dimensions. These manifolds are particularly useful for explaining how an object with more dimensions than four looks and behaves. The Calabi-Yau manifolds also gave rise to mirror symmetry, a more advanced mathematical form of symmetry.

The equations of string theory themselves are often viewed as an advancement of the field of pure mathematics. Some have even hypothesized the next advancement of string theory will be to create a new field of mathematics. This idea comes from the historical evolution of science. When Newton created gravity, he had to invent calculus to describe it. When Einstein created general relativity he had to radically alter the field of geometry. Some string theorists argue that string theory has not yet been completed because the mathematics to complete it have not yet been invented.

AdS/CFT Correspondence

An extremely important mathematical advance to come out of string theory recently is a relationship between string theory and gauge theory. This is called the Anti-de Sitter/Conformal Field Theory correspondence. Anti-de Sitter space is a particular kind of negatively curved space (so not quite like our universe, which has a slight positive curve). The conformal field theory relates to something we are already familiar with: the gauge theory of quantum physics. The gauge theory uses particles like gauge bosons to explain how forces work. Without getting into the more complicated mathematics, AdS/CFT correspondence means that there is a relationship between string theory and quantum field theories like the Standard Model. This is great news because scientists understand the Standard Model and other gauge theories quite well. And where equations in string theory may be very difficult, the corresponding equations in quantum field theory are much simpler to solve. The reverse is also true. Equations in quantum field theory that are very difficult to solve are much simpler in string theory.

This allows for major advances in both theories. Many feel that AdS/CFT correspondence is one of the most important things to come out of string theory in the last twenty years. Not only does it simplify the math required for the equations, but it also shows that there is a mathematical relationship between string theory and better understood, already accepted theories.

Extra Dimensions and Supersymmetry

String theory has lead to major breakthroughs in our understanding of extra dimensions and supersymmetry. Even if the theory does not prove useful, it is very likely that parts of it will continue to be used. This is because string theory is so versatile. It provides scientists with a set of tools that they can use to try and describe the world around them.

One of string theory's advances has been in proposing the idea of extra dimensions. String theory is not the only theory proposing other dimensions. It has, however, paved the way for physicists to think about the possibilities extra dimensions offer for physics. Scientists at the Large Hadron Collider are currently looking for extra dimensions in their particle collisions. Other theories that require extra dimensions may borrow mathematics from string theory to help describe them, like the Calabi-Yau manifolds. The search for extra dimensions may also help explain why gravity is so much weaker than the other three forces. Scientists have speculated that it is possible that gravity itself acts more heavily in other dimensions than it does in the dimensions we exist in. String theory has lead the way for research into these extra dimensions and provided ways to explain how they might work.

The 17 miles (27 km) of tunnels underground at the Large Hadron Collider are where some of the most exciting experiments in physics are happening today.

Another advance in research due to string theory has been in supersymmetry. Again, string theory is not the only proposed model of the universe to use supersymmetry, but it has done a great deal to advance our understanding of supersymmetry. Another set of experiments at the Large Hadron Collider are set to look for supersymmetrical partners that string theory and other theories first predicted. String theory, among other supersymmetry models, predicts that supersymmetrical partners may be the basis for the dark matter we observe in the universe. This would be a huge breakthrough in the understanding of dark matter, and it may lead to new interpretations of dark energy as well. Many string theorists feel that in the event string theory is disproven, it is likely that supersymmetry will still be valid and important to the future of physics.

Black Holes

Perhaps the most promising area of string theory advances is in the study of black holes. Black holes are also one of the areas that string theory set out to answer questions about by combining gravity and quantum mechanics. Amanda Peet, an influential string theorist, describes string theory like Lego® blocks. Peet uses different ideas from string theory to assemble black holes and see what their mathematics and physics look like. Scientists can create unusual or even impossible black holes to experiment with, just using the different objects of string theory and their equations. The toolkit string theory provides for this is almost endless because of the sheer number of string theories available to test.

The holographic principle is a great example of a string theory advance. The holographic principle, as a reminder, says that all the information of a three-dimensional object may be contained within the two-dimensional surface that surrounds that area. For black holes, this means that the three-dimensional matter that has disappeared could have left an impression of all its information on the boundary around the black hole. This was an advance for string theory because it helped resolve a conflict called the black hole information paradox. Not only did the holographic principle revolutionize black holes in string theory, but it is a huge development for the study of black holes in general. Some string theorists feel that the holographic principle may end up being one of the key features of M-theory as well.

LOOP QUANTUM GRAVITY

The alternative to string theory is one most people probably have not heard of. This is for a few reasons. It is not quite as engaging a theory. Loop quantum gravity has no extra dimensions and no holograms, and it makes no attempts to

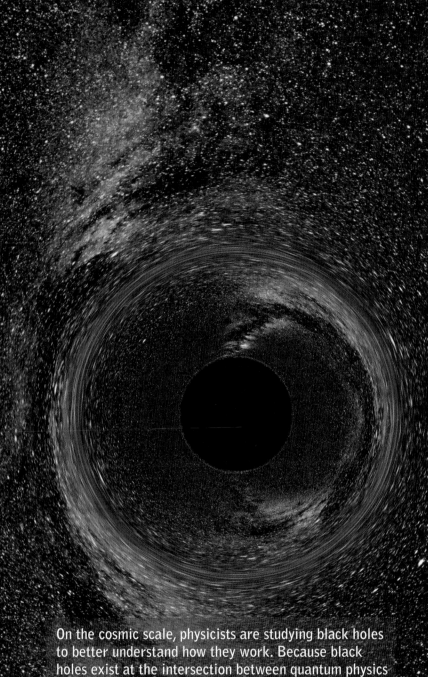

On the cosmic scale, physicists are studying black holes
to better understand how they work. Because black
holes exist at the intersection between quantum physics
and general relativity, understanding them may lead
to major breakthroughs in string theory and a unified
theory of everything.

become a theory of everything. It is also string theory's main opposition for becoming a theory of quantum gravity. Like string theory there are several things in its favor and several flaws it still has to work out. At its heart, loop quantum gravity is a new way of thinking about space on the scale of particles and atoms. It does have in its favor that it is a background-independent theory. This means that loop quantum gravity does not require a fixed background. This makes it distinctly different from string theory and the Standard Model. It also allows loop quantum gravity to be a better approximation of the theory of general relativity on a quantum scale.

An important note about loop quantum gravity: it does not set out to become a theory of everything. It does not unite the four forces in the way that string theory does. It is only seeking to describe space and gravity on the scale of quantum mechanics. This is one of the reasons that it gets less press, its proponents argue, but it also makes it a less far-reaching theory.

Quantized Space

Loop quantum gravity seeks to explain gravity on the quantum scale by quantizing space. The Standard Model, covered earlier, says that energy comes in individual units, or quanta. Loop quantum gravity says that space also comes in quanta. This is an unusual way of thinking about space and allows for some cool things to happen in the mathematics because of it. Remember that deformations in space-time, according to Einstein, are what cause gravity. So loop quantum gravity sets out to explain space on the quantum scale, and by doing that, it also explain quantum gravity.

Imagine space is a fabric. Like a fabric, on very close inspection, space could be made of threads. These threads of space are woven together. The connections between the threads are where space is quantized, or comes in discrete bundles. It is interesting that when physicists set out to find the equations for quantized space, particles came out in the mathematics. In the same way string theorists set out to describe particle interactions they discovered a graviton in their equations.

Predictions

Loop quantum gravity supporters will say this is the most important difference between loop quantum gravity and string theory: it makes predictions. The problem is they are not really testable predictions yet. But they are at least some predictions.

The first is that gravity exists on the quantum scale as a deformation of space. This is the same way gravity works on larger scales according to general relativity. One problem with this is that it is yet to be proven that general relativity functions the same way on the quantum scale and with the same numbers. It's not clear yet how this quantized space looks on larger scales.

It also predicts that a special type of high-energy radiation should move faster than other types of radiation. This phenomenon is called doubly special relativity. This is not a violation of the constant speed of light because that only applies in a true vacuum. In reality, space is not a pure vacuum so doubly special relativity technically does not violate the speed of light in a vacuum. If loop quantum gravity's hypothesis is correct, gamma ray bursts coming from far-away supernovae will have different photons moving at different speeds. So far, there has been no evidence of differing speeds in the light we detect from these supernovae, though the calculations for the probability of these events say we should have observed these by now.

Another important prediction it has made is the entropy level (or the level of chaos) inside of a black hole and the Hawking radiation coming out of it. The entropy level loop quantum gravity predicts lines up with the predictions made by other scientists, lending credence to loop quantum gravity.

Flaws

Loop quantum gravity is not without flaws. Scientists have yet to come up with good experimental tests to show whether or not it is correct. The same problems that plague string theory's testability are also present in loop quantum gravity. The size of the space being described is currently beyond our ability to test. However there are perhaps more tests available to loop quantum gravity because it has more predictions than string theory.

It also currently does not have time involved with the quantized space. In order for loop quantum gravity to become a quantum theory of general relativity, it will have to allow for both space and time in its background. Lee Smolin, one of the foremost loop quantum gravity theorists, believes that time will become fundamental in the equations but this has not happened yet.

One of the largest problems outside of the search for doubly special relativity is that it does not make any new testable predictions that the Standard Model or general relativity did not make. This is the same problem that plagues string theory currently.

Perhaps most importantly, loop quantum gravity has yet to show that you can have quantized space on the small scale that leads to a smooth fabric of space on the large scale. One of the requirements of general relativity is a smooth space-time fabric on the scale of planets and stars. If loop quantum gravity does not yield a smooth fabric of space-time it will be in serious trouble as a theory of quantum gravity and general relativity.

BOTH THEORIES of QUANTUM GRAVITY

There is some shared ground between the two theories of quantum gravity. Both of them discovered something unexpected while trying to describe something else. When string theorists set out to explain particle interactions, gravity fell out of their equations. And when loop quantum gravity set out to explain how quantum space works, particles fell out.

Both theories accurately predicted the entropy inside black holes and Hawking radiation coming out of them. The fact that both theories, using various assumptions, managed to predict a number that was established already is important. It suggests that they are on the right track for predicting other things about black holes that will be correct.

Some physicists wonder if there is a correspondence or duality within string theory and loop quantum gravity. A duality, as a reminder, means that there are two different ways of viewing the same event. There is a remote possibility that the compactified dimensions from string theory could be equal to the quantized space units of loop quantum gravity. As loop quantum gravity is developed, string theorists may be able to incorporate quantized space into string theory. Both theories are still incomplete, so it could be that this is not the case.

String theorists and the physicists working on loop quantum gravity accuse each other of groupthink. Groupthink means that scientists do not have critical discourse. Scientists need to have constructive and critical conversations in order to advance the field. If no one ever challenges certain views, the field never grow and no new ideas will be made. Without critical discourse among string theorists, loop quantum gravity proponents, and other physicists, science fails to advance.

STRING THEORY and the HISTORY of SCIENCE

Because it is still uncertain what string theory will or will not lead to, its place in the history of science is unclear. There are three options for how physicists will view string theory in one hundred years. The first, worst-case scenario, is that supersymmetry or extra dimensions are somehow disproven and the entirety of string theory is wrong. In this case scientists would likely view string theory in the same way they view the theory of luminiferous ether. It would be seen as an idea that people refused to give up in spite of all evidence to the contrary.

The second and third cases are more positive. In the second scenario some parts of string theory are disproven, but not essential parts. String theorists are still able to use pieces of the equations to describe other events in physics, and it lives on in a way but does not fill its potential as a theory of everything. The third scenario is that scientists complete the equations to describe our universe and find evidence of string theory that supports its predictions. This scenario is what most string theorists are hoping for, but it may never come to be.

In the history of gravity there have been many revisions. Newton first described gravity in his laws of motion. He did more than this, though, because he unified gravity on Earth and gravity in the heavens. Next up was Einstein and his theory of general relativity, unifying space and time with gravity. String theory is the result of a search for a third revision of gravity: gravity on the scale of atoms and particles. Scientists do not know if string theory, loop quantum gravity, or some other yet-to-be-described theory of quantum gravity will end up being correct. It could be that we are never able to prove any one theory over another.

String theory is also a great example in the history of science of physicists and mathematicians cooperating together. The last time mathematicians had so much to do with theoretical physics was perhaps during the work of Faraday and Maxwell. Thanks to the weird and wonderful consequences of string theory, the field of pure mathematics has advanced by leaps and bounds.

One of the most important things in science is learning from your mistakes. Isaac Asimov, a biochemist and writer, said, "The most exciting phrase to hear in science, the one that heralds new discoveries, is not 'Eureka!' but 'That's funny...'" If string theory is proven incorrect, the ways that it is wrong will probably be more interesting than the fact that it is wrong.

One of the reasons scientists use computer mathematical models of a system (like a black hole or even a rain forest habitat) is to compare reality to the model. When scientists create the model, they find values for factors they think are important. In the computer model, they will weigh these things more heavily. When the computer model is wrong is when interesting science happens. It is from these errors in their thinking that scientists can learn the most. It is important that string theory has given us a way to model particle physics, black holes, and the big bang. Even if it is wrong, we will learn from where it was wrong. String theory may be like the Michelson-Morley experiment at work. Even though Michelson and Morley did not discover what they had hoped to, the results of their work revolutionized physics.

While it is not clear whether or not string theory will ever be solved for our universe, or if it is even correct, its place in the history of science cannot be denied. For the last forty years string theory has managed to survive through every challenge thrown at it. This is important in and of itself, and string theorists argue it lends credibility to the theory.

WHAT'S NEXT?

String theory has undergone many, many revisions, starting first from Veneziano's work describing collisions using Euler's equations all the way through Ed Witten uniting all five string theories into M-theory. As we have delved deeper into the mathematics of string theory our understanding of it has changed. We now understand that there are almost limitless versions of the theory. This is both astonishing and disheartening, depending on your view. It is unlikely at this point that string theorists will find the numbers that make string theory describe our unique universe. But it also allows

$E=mc^2$ is the mathematical equation in Albert Einstein's theory of special relativity.

for us to explore a variety of universes that could exist through string theory.

The major question for many is how we will answer the question of quantum gravity and Einstein's quest for a unified theory of everything. Loop quantum gravity poses some new answers, but it also falls short in uniting the four forces into a single set of equations. String theory has large goals, but they may be unreachable. But using string theory as a mathematical model for the world has lead to advances in pure mathematics. It brings new understanding to the Standard Model through AdS/CFT correspondence. And it creates a toolkit to examine events like the big bang and black holes.

The horizon of string theory is like the theory itself: full of possibilities. It could be that the Large Hadron Collider in Europe never finds evidence of supersymmetry, which would discredit string theory. Maybe extra dimensions are found in some of these same collisions at the LHC. It could be that as we look more into black holes, the holographic principle is disproven or that loop quantum gravity is found to contain infinite mathematical terms, which would invalidate it as a theory of quantum gravity.

One thing is for sure: physicists will continue Einstein's quest for the ultimate theory of everything. This is the next great frontier of science. Where it will lead us is not certain, but the discoveries of this quest will be monumental. Whether or not string theory is the answer to that quest is still to be determined.

Chronology

1865   James Clerk Maxwell describes the equations for electromagnetism

1887   Michelson-Morley experiments report that light is the same no matter how it is observed (most scientists believe the experiments must have been flawed somehow)

1900   Max Planck hypothesizes that all particles have a particular amount of energy

1905   Albert Einstein publishes the theory of special relativity, the dual nature of light, and another paper on blackbody radiation

1916   Albert Einstein publishes the theory of general relativity, unifying gravity and relativity

1927   Werner Heisenberg describes the uncertainty principle

1964   Murray Gell-Mann suggests the quark model

1968   Gabriele Veneziano proposes the dual resonance
          model to explain particle interactions

1970   Yoichiro Nambu, Holger Nielsen, and Leonard
          Susskind each independently propose the dual
          resonance model is a model describing small, vibrating
          strings

1971   Pierre Ramond proposes supersymmetry and creates
          superstring theory

1974   Joël Scherk and John Schwarz come up with string
          theory as a theory of quantum gravity

1984   The first superstring revolution is started by Michael
          Green and John Schwarz when they remove anomalies
          from string theory mathematics

1985   The Princeton String Quartet develops heterotic string
          theory; Ed Witten and others begin describing the
          Calabi-Yau manifolds

1995   Ed Witten gives his talk about M-theory and starts
          the second superstring revolution; Joseph Polchinski
          proposes strings can end on D-branes

Glossary

atom The smallest unit of an element. The name comes from the Greek word "atomos," which means uncuttable, and was proposed to be the smallest possible unit of matter. The atom is made up of protons, neutrons, and electrons.

black hole Something so massive it distorts the space-time around it so much that not even light can escape its gravity. Black holes are one of the prime areas of research for a unified theory of everything because they are both massive and very small. This means they require gravity and quantum mechanics.

boson A group of subatomic particles with whole integer spin that are the force carriers for the four fundamental forces. The Higgs boson, which was long theorized, was finally discovered in 2012. String theorists hope to one day discover evidence of a graviton, the proposed gauge boson responsible for the force of gravity.

brane Integral part of M-theory. Branes can have three or more dimensions and interact with open strings. Certain types of branes are used to explain black holes in string theory.

charge A fundamental characteristic of a particle that dictates its interactions with other particles. Charge can refer to electrical charge (positive or negative) or color charge (red, green, or blue). Electrical charge is responsible for electromagnetism, while color charge is responsible for the interaction of quarks.

duality A mathematical principle where one event can be viewed and described in two distinctly different ways.

electricity The effect of electrically charged particles and the way they direct energy flow; a result of the electromagnetic force.

electromagnetic force The force that is responsible for electricity and magnetism. It is the result of particles being repulsed or attracted to each other as a result of their charge. The flow of electricity creates an electrical current and a magnetic field. This is one of the four basic forces of physics.

electron A subatomic particle that has negative charge and resides in an orbit cloud around the nucleus of an atom. Electrons are in the lepton group of subatomic particles. They are elementary and can't be broken down further. Electrons respond to the electromagnetic and gravitational forces.

element A substance that cannot be broken down into pieces by chemical means. An element is defined by the number of protons in its nucleus, and it has a matching number of electrons in its electron cloud.

fermion A subatomic particle class that has half integer spin and mass. These are the particles that are responsible for matter. Fermions can have both electrical charge and color charge. Fermions include other groups of subatomic particles, like leptons, hadrons, and quarks.

force Any one of the four natural phenomena that describe interactions possible between matter on everything from the scale of subatomic particles to galaxies. They include the gravitational force, the electromagnetic force, the weak nuclear force, and the strong nuclear force.

general relativity Einstein's theory of gravity. It uses the distortion of an object on the fabric of space-time to explain the gravitational force. General relativity is fundamentally incompatible with our modern understanding of the standard model of quantum physics.

gluon A subatomic particle in the boson class. It has color charge and is the particle responsible for carrying for the strong force.

gravitational force One of the fundamental forces that relates to the attraction between any two objects. The strength of gravity increases with mass of the objects and decreases with the distance between them. It is the weakest of the fundamental forces.

hadron A class of subatomic fermion particle that is made up of quarks. It has half-integer spin and is capable of carrying electrical charge. Neutrons and protons are both examples of hadrons.

holographic principle A mathematical principle that states all the information of a three-dimensional object can be contained within a two-dimensional boundary. In M-theory it resolves the black hole information paradox.

Large Hadron Collider The largest particle accelerator in the world, located on the border of France and Switzerland. The collider consists of 17 miles of underground tunnels that form the track for the collider. The LHC is an effort of CERN, the European Organization for Nuclear Research. It is the major center for experimental particle physics and capable of very high-energy particle collisions.

lepton A group of subatomic fermion particles with the ability to carry charge. Examples of leptons include electrons and the various types of neutrinos. They interact through the gravitational and electromagnetic forces.

M-theory Created by Ed Witten, this new version of string theory was a unification of the five string theories from the first superstring revolution. It has eleven dimensions of space and time, branes, and strings.

neutron A subatomic particle with neutral electrical charge found in the nucleus of an atom. It is a hadron particle made up of two up quarks and one down quark. Neutrons can break down through the weak force into other particles as a process of nuclear decay.

particle See subatomic particle.

particle accelerator A machine that uses magnets to accelerate subatomic particles to immense speeds and then records results of high-speed collisions between subatomic particles. Particle accelerators are the major experimental tool for quantum physicists. Today the largest particle accelerator in the world is the Large Hadron Collider at CERN in Geneva, Switzerland.

photon The force-carrying particle of the electromagnetic force. It can travel as a wave or a particle and has no mass or electric charge. Photons travel at a constant speed of approximately 3×10^8 meters per second in a vacuum.

physics The study of matter and its interactions and how the universe behaves. The science of the subatomic world is called quantum physics, while the science of celestial bodies and the universe is called cosmology. All different parts of physics involve the study of the fundamental forces of the universe.

proton A hadron subatomic particle made up of two down quarks and one up quark. It is located within the nucleus of an atom. The number of protons in the nucleus determines its chemical element. The proton carries a positive electric charge.

quantum (plural quanta) The smallest discrete unit of energy that can exist. First hypothesized by Max Planck, the idea that matter and energy exist in distinct units became the basis for quantum physics and subatomic research.

quantum mechanics A branch of physics that deals with subatomic particles and their interactions. The behavior of the particles or quanta is described using probabilities that they will interact one way versus another. One of the largest challenges facing quantum mechanics today is that it is incompatible with Einstein's theory of general relativity and gravity.

quark A type of subatomic fermion that carries color charge. These are the only fermions that interact using the strong force. The strong force holds quarks together to create hadrons like neutrons and protons. Quarks are never experimentally observed outside of a hadron particle. They come in six flavors: up, down, bottom, top, strange, and charm.

space-time The concept Einstein introduced to physics to explain the way gravity works. To understand gravity, Einstein equated space and time and related them together. In order for gravity to work, space-time must be smooth and changeable.

special relativity Einstein's concept to explain the constant speed of light in a vacuum. It is a special case of motion because it only relates to objects in motion but not accelerating. Special relativity says that before one comments on the motion of another system one must state what one believes one's own motion to be. It is also the theory that says there is an equivalence between an object's mass and its speed, giving rise to the equation $E=mc^2$.

strong force The force responsible for holding quarks together to create hadrons. Particles interacting through the strong force have color charge. The gluon is the force carrier for the strong force. This is the strongest of the four physical forces of the universe.

subatomic particle Any of the various pieces of matter that make up part of the atom. Subatomic particles include hadrons like neutrons and protons, leptons like electrons and neutrinos, and quarks like up and down. They also include the particles that carry force like gluons and photons.

supersymmetry A concept in physics that states that for every described particle there is a superpartner that is identical except for one characteristic that is opposite. The superpartner of a fermion starts with an "s" (an electron's superparter would be a selectron) and the superpartner of a boson ends with "ino" (the superpartner of a photon is a photino).

weak force The force responsible for nuclear decay and radiation. The force carriers of the weak force are the W⁺, W⁻, and Z bosons. The particles of the weak force are extremely massive, and they break down almost instantly.

Further Information

BOOKS

Greene, Brian. *The Elegant Universe*. New York, NY: W. W. Norton & Company, 2003.

Gribbin, John. *Get a Grip on Physics*. New York, NY: Metro Books, 1999.

Lane, Shaun Michael. Is the Universe Really Made of Tiny Rubber Bands?. Walnut, CA: MSAC Philosophy Group, 2014.

Zimmerman Jones, Andrew. *String Theory for Dummies*. Hoboken, NJ: Wiley Publishing, 2010.

WEBSITES

The Official String Theory Website
superstringtheory.com

A more in-depth guide to the mathematics and physics involved in string theory.

Why String Theory?
www.whystringtheory.com

A website supported by the University of Oxford and the Royal Society that gives easy-to-understand explanations of string theory as well as updates on string theory research.

VIDEOS

The Elegant Universe
www.pbs.org/wgbh/nova/physics/elegant-universe.html

This 2003 NOVA special produced by PBS stars Brian Greene and is based on his book of the same name.

String Theory and the Hidden Structure of Space-time
https://www.youtube.com/watch?v=olabyP4zfGg

Another short but notable TED talk by Dr. Spenta Wadia. It gives a brief overview of quantum physics and gravity and what string theory brings to our understanding of both.

Visualizing Eleven Dimensions
https://www.youtube.com/watch?v=aSz5BjExs9o

A short TED talk by Thad Roberts about how to visualize eleven dimensions and how they might work.

Atiyah, Michael. "On the Work of Edward Witten." Proceedings of the International Congress of Mathematicians, Kyoto, Japan, 1990.

Barrow, John D., and John D. Barrow. *New Theories of Everything: The Quest for Ultimate Explanation.* Oxford: Oxford University Press, 2007.

Becker, Katrin, Melanie Becker, and John H. Schwarz. *String Theory and M-theory: A Modern Introduction.* Cambridge: Cambridge University Press, 2007.

Bennett, Jeffrey. *What Is Relativity? An Intuitive Introduction to Einstein's Ideas and Why They Matter.* New York, NY: Columbia University Press, 2014.

Biography.com. "Leonhard Euler: Biography" (http://www.biography.com/people/leonhard-euler-21342391).

CalTech Oral Histories. John H. Schwarz interview by Sara Lippincott. Pasadena, CA, July 21 and 26, 2000. Oral History Project, California Institute of Technology Archives (http://resolver.caltech.edu/CaltechOH:OH_Schwarz_J).

Callahan, James. *The Geometry of Spacetime: An Introduction to Special and General Relativity*. New York: Springer, 2000.

Centre for Inquiry. "String Theory for the Scientifically Curious with Dr. Amanda Peet." July 10, 2012 (https://www.youtube.com/watch?v=PpQngpaHamg).

CERN. "The Higgs Boson" (http://www.home.cern/topics/higgs-boson).

CERN. "The Large Hadron Collider" (http://www.home.cern/topics/large-hadron-collider).

CERN. "The Standard Model" (http://www.home.cern/about/physics/standard-model).Chown, Marcus. The Quantum Zoo: A Tourist's Guide to the Neverending Universe. Washington, DC: Joseph Henry Press, 2006.

Conlon, Joseph, Charlotte Mason, and Edward Hughes. "Why String Theory? A Layman's Journey to the Frontiers of Physics" (http://www.whystringtheory.com).

Diem-Lane, Shaun-Michael. "String Theory for Kids." YouTube. March 18, 2015. Accessed May 2, 2016. https://www.youtube.com/watch?v=SXqvwGT819w.

The Edge. "The Landscape: A Talk with Leonard Susskind." 2003 (http://www.edge.org/3rd_culture/susskind03/susskind_index.html).

Floating University. "Michio Kaku Explains String Theory." December 11, 2011 (http://www.youtube.com/watch?v=kYAdwS5MfjQ).

Gamow, George. *The Great Physicists from Galileo to Einstein.* New York, NY: Dover Publications, 1988.

Greene, Brian. *The Elegant Universe: Superstrings, Hidden Dimensions, and the Quest for the Ultimate Theory.* New York, NY: W. W. Norton & Company, 2003.

Greene, Brian. *The Fabric of the Cosmos: Space, Time, and the Texture of Reality.* New York, NY: Vintage Books, 2004.

Greene, Brian. *The Hidden Reality: Parallel Universe and the Deep Laws of the Cosmos.* New York, NY: Vintage Books, 2011.

Gribbin, John. *Get a Grip on Physics.* New York, NY: Metro Books, 1999.

Gubser, Steven S. *The Little Book of String Theory.* Princeton, NJ: Princeton University Press, 2010.

Jones, Andrew Zimmerman, and Daniel Robbins. *String Theory for Dummies.* Hoboken, NJ: Wiley Publishing, 2010.

Kaku, Michio. Official Website of Dr. Michio Kaku (http://mkaku.org).

Kaku, Michio. "Michio Kaku Explains String Theory." YouTube. December 07, 2011. Accessed May 03, 2016. https://www.youtube.com/watch?v=kYAdwS5MFjQ.

Kaku, Michio. *Parallel Worlds: A Journey through Creation, Higher Dimensions, and the Future of the Cosmos.* New York: Doubleday, 2015.

Mukhi, Sunil. "String Theory and the Unification of Forces." October 7, 2000 (http://www.theory.tifr.res.in/~mukhi/Physics/string.html).

Mukhi, Sunil. "The Theory of Strings: A Detailed Introduction." October 9, 1999 (http://www.theory.tifr.res.in/~mukhi/Physics/string2.html).

Particle Adventure: The Fundamentals of Matter and Force (http://www.particleadventure.org/index.html).

PBS.org. "The Elegant Universe." NOVA, 2012 (http://www.pbs.org/wgbh/nova/physics/elegant-universe.html#elegant-universe).

PBS.org. "The Fabric of the Cosmos." NOVA, 2011 (http://www.pbs.org/wgbh/nova/physics/fabric-of-cosmos.html). Perimeter Institute for Theoretical Physics. "Perimeter Public Lecture: String Theory Legos for Black Holes." May 8, 2015 (https://www.youtube.com/watch?v=MlDd2HtFfPU).

Pickover, Clifford A. *The Physics Devotional.* New York, NY: Sterling. 2015.

Polchinski, Joseph Gerard. *String Theory*. Cambridge: Cambridge University Press, 2005.

Robbins, Louise E., ed. *The American Heritage Student Science Dictionary. Second edition*. Boston, MA: Houghton Mifflin Harcourt, 2014.

Roberts, Thad, and Jeff Chapple. *Einstein's Intuition: Visualizing Nature in Eleven Dimensions*.

Schwarz, John H. "Reminiscences of Collaborations with Joël Scherk." Paper presented at the Conférence anniversaire du LPT-ENS, July 14, 2000.

Schwarz, Patricia. The Official String Theory Website (http://www.superstringtheory.com).

Schwarz, Patricia M., and John H. Schwarz. *Special Relativity: From Einstein to Strings*. Combridge, U.K.: Cambridge University Press, 2004.

Silicon Valley Astronomy Lectures. "The Black Hole Wars: My Battle with Stephen Hawking," October 1, 2008. Posted September 4, 2013 (http://www.youtube.com/watch?v=KR3Msi1YeXQ).

Smolin, Lee. *The Trouble with Physics: The Rise of String Theory, the Fall of a Science, and What Comes Next*. New York, NY: Houghton Mifflin, 2007.

Suskind, Leonard. *The Cosmic Landscape: String Theory and the Illusion of Intelligent Design*. New York: Little and Brown, 2005.

TED.com. "Brian Greene: Making Sense of String Theory." Filmed February 2005. TED Talk, 19:06 (http://www.ted.com/talks/brian_greene_on_string_theory?language=en).

Wadia, Spenta. "String Theory and the Hidden Structure of Space-time | Dr. Spenta Wadia | TEDxStXaviersMumbai." YouTube. May 27, 2015. Accessed May 03, 2016. https://www.youtube.com/watch?v=olabyP4zfGg.

Whitwell, Tim. "What Is String Theory?" (http://www.physics.org/article-questions.asp?id=47).

Why String Theory. "AdS-CFT: Through the Looking Glass" (http://www.whystringtheory.com/toolbox/ads-cft/).

Yau, Shing-Tung, and Steven Nadis. *The Shape of Inner Space: String Theory and the Geometry of the Universe's Hidden Dimensions*. New York: Basic Books, 2010.

Page numbers in **boldface** are illustrations. Entries in **boldface** are glossary terms.

dimensions
in bosonic string theory,
52, 55
in superstring theory, 55,
58, 64, 66, 67, 69–70, 71,
77, 78, 91, 92, 96, 101
duality, 18–19
dual resonance model, 50, 51,
52, 53, 54, 57

Earth, 10, 14, 38, 39, 67, 79,
102
E8xE8 symmetry, 64
E= mc2, 18, 42, **104**
Einstein, Albert, 15, 29, **37**,
38, 39, 57
theory of general relativity,
5, 6, 19–20, 24, 25, 27,
36, 45, 74, 93, 102
theory of special relativity,
17–18, 36
unified theory of
everything, 6, 24, 36, 81,
105
electricity, 11–14, 40
electromagnetic force, 11–14,
17, 19, 21, **23**, 24, 29, 33,
35, 38, 39–41, 53
electron, 5, 19, 21, 28, 29, 30,
32, 40, 41, 52, 53, 55, 57
discovery of, 27–28
electron neutrino, 32
element, 5, 21, 29, 42
energy, vibrating, **4**, 5, **22**, 52,
62, 63, 64, 67

Euler, Leonhard, 6, 47–48, **49**,
50, 51, 61, 103
Euler beta functions, 48, 50,
51
European Organization for
Nuclear Research (CERN),
50, 57
event horizon, 78

Faraday, James, 11–13, 21, 25,
40, 41, 102
Faraday's law of induction, 12
fermion, 31–32, 44, 53, 55,
57, 72
Feynman, 35, 39
forces, description of the four,
35–44

gauge theory, 33, 93
Gell-Mann, Murray, 54
general relativity, theory of,
5, 19–20, 24, 25, 27, 36, 45,
74, 78, 83, 85, 87, 93, 98,
100, 102
Gliozzi, Ferdinando, 57
glueball, 44
gluon, 33, 35, 44, 72
gravitational force, 10, 11, 21,
23, 25, **34**, 35, 38–39, 42,
44, 45, 48, 56, 65–66, 77,
79, 80, 81
and Einstein, 5, 6, 19–20,
24, 38–39
and Newton, 10, 11, 20, 93,
102

nuclear fission, 48
nuclear fusion, 42
nuclear power, 23
nucleus, 21, 23, **28**, 29, 32, 35,
    40, 43, 44, 50

Olive, David, 57
O (32) symmetry group, 64
oxygen, 5, 29

particle accelerator, 6, 32, 33,
    48, 50, 52, 77, 81, 94, **95**,
    105
particles, what they are, 21
particle/wave duality, 18–19,
    36
p-brane, 74, 77
photon, 19, 29, 33, 41, 53, 55,
    72
physics, what it is, 9
Planck, Max, 19, 20, 25, 29
polarization, 41
Polchinski, Joseph, 60
Princeton String Quartet, 58,
    59
probability, and quantum
    physics, 23
proton, 5, 1, **28**, 29, **30**, 32, **33**,
    40, 41, 42, 43, 44, 53, 66
pure mathematics, 48, 91, 93,
    105

quantum, 19
quantum chromodynamics,
    52

quantum gravity, 45, 56, 57,
    58, 63, 66, 80, 83, 87, 88,
    96, 98–101, 102
quantum mechanics, 5, 6, 7,
    25, 48, 53, 63, 65–66, 67,
    69, 73, 81, 85
    establishment of field,
        20–21, 23–24
quark, 5, 31, 32, 33, 35, 42,
    43, 44

Ramond, Pierre, 55
Rohm, Ryan, 58

Scherk, Joël, 55–57
Schwarz, John, 55, **56**, 57, 58,
    63, 72
scientific method, what it is,
    16, 73
S-duality, 65
Silverstein, Eva, 57
solar eclipse, 39, 74
space-time, 38, 39, 48, 87, 98,
    100
special relativity, **theory** of,
    17–18, 36
speed of light, 14, 17, 18, 19,
    52, 57
spin
    ½ integer, 31
    2-spin, 35, 39
    whole integer, 31, 32
    0-spin, 35
Stanford University, 52

About the Author

Meghan Rock is a scientific writer and illustrator. Her background includes art, writing, and invertebrate biology, but quantum physics and cosmology have always been a passion of hers. Her illustration work has been used in presentations and papers the world over and spans the range from invertebrate biology to forensic science. She lives in Chicago, where she enjoys hiking with her dog, teaching art to young students, going to museums, and reading in the company of her cat. One of her dreams is to travel to Geneva, Switzerland, to tour the Large Hadron Collider at CERN.